THE NEW CONCERT OF NATIONS

The New Concert of Nations

A BACKGROUND BOOK

C. M. Woodhouse

DUFOUR EDITIONS
CHESTER SPRINGS
PENNSYLVANIA

CONTENTS

I

The Sources of Disequilibrium

TWO IDEAS, both of them unprecedented in human history, to-day dominate international relations. It is my purpose here to examine them and their consequences. One is the idea that it is wrong for any people to be subject to any other people; and this is called *anti-colonialism*. The other idea is that there is a moral obligation, absolute and unconditional, upon richer nations to help poorer nations to reach a higher standard of living; and this is called *aid to under-developed countries*. A few essential qualifications apart, these two ideas are now universally taken for granted, both by public opinion and by governments, both in the older and richer countries and in the newer and poorer ones, with an assurance which almost entirely overlooks their very paradoxical character.

The paradox is not, as it is sometimes represented, that the two ideas are mutually incompatible. It is true that there is an element of inconsistency between the equally compelling desires of the under-developed countries to which these ideas respond: the desire to be helped to a higher standard of living, and the desire to be left alone without foreign interference.

It is also arguable that the motives of the richer countries in helping the under-developed countries are not always so disinterested as they make out. There is nevertheless a strong element of pure philanthropy in them, and an even stronger disinclination, at least among the western powers, ever to be induced to intervene again in Asia or Africa in an imperialist fashion. Even without that disinclination, there are forces at work in the world to-day which make a return to imperialism along the road of economic aid unthinkable. What is paradoxical about the two ideas which are now universally accepted is therefore something quite different. It is rather that they run counter to all past human experience.

They have only become widely accepted as ideas in the course of the present century; and this raises the question how durable they are likely to prove.

Throughout the millennia of human history until the 20th century, the exact opposite of these two ideas was taken for granted, just as unquestioningly. To the conqueror went the spoils, and the weakest went to the wall. Great powers were expected to overrun small powers and to exploit them for their own benefit. Some may have questioned whether this was morally right, but no one disputed that it was natural. And imperialism of this kind lasted well into the present century. It was the philosophy of Cecil Rhodes, Marshal Lyautey and Kaiser Wilhelm, all of whom regarded themselves as benefactors of the people they sought to dominate.

Imperialism as an idea is still not entirely defunct, but it is nowadays contrary to the spirit of the times. The Portuguese still practise the traditional doctrine in Africa, as also do the Afrikaner Nationalists in the South African Republic. The non-Communist countries accuse the Russians of old-fashioned imperialism in Central Asia and even in Eastern Europe; and they accuse the Chinese of the same offence in South-East Asia. Less conspicuously, the withdrawal of European imperialism from Asia and Africa has left behind many lesser peoples subject to more dominant peoples—Karens and Shans subject to Burmans, Kurds to Iraqis, Nagas to Indians, Ashanti to Ghanaians, and so on.

These relationships might on a strict interpretation be

held to infringe the doctrine of self-determination, but they seem not to be so offensive to the collective conscience of contemporary humanity because they do not involve European colonisation. They are accepted as nothing worse than marginal qualifications to an uncontested general rule.

They do indeed show, however, that a perfect rearrangement of political sovereignty in the world is a delusion. History will not come to a full stop in an ideal dispensation, as only the most doctrinaire Marxists still believe it will. There are many absurdities about the present distribution of sovereignty in the world: gigantic states like India exercising the same voice in the United Nations as minute states like Kuweit; even tinier relics of independence like San Marino or Abu Dhabi; states which consist of arbitrary lines drawn on the map, like Jordan, and states equally arbitrarily cut in half, like Korea and Vietnam.

But imperfect as the present dispensation is, the probability is that the pattern which it presents on the map will not greatly change, if at all, in the foreseeable future. There is scarcely anywhere a real vacuum that remains to be filled; and any temptation to try to change the existing pattern is likely to be frustrated by the world-wide prejudice in favour of the two ideas with which I began—the idea of anti-colonialism and the sense of international obligation towards the small, the poor and the weak.

These two currently dominant ideas have, however, an extremely short history behind them. So dominant are they to-day that it is difficult to recall how short a time ago they would have seemed absurd to all but a high-minded minority among the western races, and unattainable to all but a sophisticated few among the victims of colonial oppression.

When the principle of self-determination was proclaimed by President Wilson in the First World War, no one seriously thought of applying it outside Europe. Even in the Second World War, the colonies of the European powers were not generally thought to come within the scope of the Atlantic Charter. Winston Churchill said in 1942 that he had not become the King's first minister in order to preside over the liquidation of the British Empire. The Socialist government of 1945 included no reference to the coming independence of the British Colonies in its policy statements, either before or immediately after its election, because at the beginning of its term no one contemplated such an outcome.

Although the Second World War was in fact the watershed over which both ideas poured in a growing cataract, their inevitability was only slowly recognised. The idea of colonial independence was at first stubbornly resisted: by the Dutch in Indonesia, by the French in Indo-China, by the British in Africa even after they had accepted it in India. What was strange about the growth of the idea was its relatively slow emergence into conscious form: it had come to stay long before it was recognised.

The British presided over the liquidation of other nations' empires, and even over the Asian parts of their own, without at first appreciating the logical sequel that must follow in Africa and everywhere else. As late as 1954 a British Minister could say in the House of Commons that 'it has always been understood and agreed that there are certain territories in the Commonwealth which, owing to their particular circumstances, can never expect to be fully independent'. He was speaking in the context of Cyprus, which became independent six years later; but no one contested that there were some territories to which his words still applied. To-day it would be much more vigorously questioned whether there are any.

The other idea, that of an obligation to aid under-developed countries, grew even more slowly. Like the idea of independence, it had its origins in the Second World War: it was a sort of extension of the principles of the Welfare State at home.

Characteristically, the first steps were taken by the British government at one of the darkest moments of the war, when the first Colonial Development and Welfare Act was passed in 1940; and the Colonial Development Corporation was created in 1947. But the new tide of thinking took many years to gather force, and still longer to become the unchallengeable dogma which it now is. Of the corresponding French institutions, FIDES (*Fonds d'Investissement pour le Développement Économique et Social*) has directed its resources exclusively to French overseas territories only since 1959, and the *Fonds d'Aide et de Co-opération*, confined to the French African territories, was founded only in the same year.

The Americans launched their vast programme of overseas aid at first in forms very different from those which it was later to take: European countries, not under-developed territories, were the first recipients, and military support was the major feature of it.

Even to-day the direction of much US aid is determined by strategic considerations. Among the largest recipients, for instance, are the three rump territories in the Far East left over by civil wars—Formosa, South Korea and the remains of ex-French Indo-China. Only in the late 1950s, when the risk of a Third World War began to recede, did the American government begin to act on the purely humanitarian assumption that under-developed countries must be helped to a better life for its own sake, whether or not they were threatened by Communism.

It would be wrong to heap scorn on the Americans for

this belated recognition. The United Nations itself was very little in advance of the US government along the same line of thought in the post-war years. Its Technical Assistance Board, which was the first move in the direction of aid to under-developed countries, was set up only in 1950, and the Special Fund not until 1958. The World Bank began lending to under-developed countries only late in the 1950s, having previously concentrated on helping relatively advanced countries which were under-developed only in the economist's technical sense, such as Australia, Italy, South Africa and Japan. The idea of an obligation to aid the poorer countries of the world now has such a grip on the imagination of us all that it is difficult to remember how new an idea it is.

For the same reason, it is difficult to judge how durable it will be. Will its fate be like that of the seeds which fell on stony ground and 'forthwith they sprung up because they had no deepness of earth', only to wither away when the sun was up?

It must be recognised at least that the present mood of the richer nations is one that runs counter to the whole of previous human history, and owes its origin to a conjunction of circumstances which is unlikely to continue indefinitely. The most important element in it is a guilty conscience. The western capitalist powers, commonly called the colonial or imperialist powers, feel an obligation to make restitution to the peoples whom they once exploited, and to tolerate almost any degree of unreasonable behaviour by those peoples as excusable in the light of their past oppression.

The Americans, though never strictly speaking an imperialist people, share in the guilty conscience, perhaps not so much because theirs is a capitalist economy but rather because they too have been guilty of racial domination directed against the negroes in their midst. The

Soviet Russians, though increasingly prosperous and constantly accused of imperialism by their enemies, have escaped the stigma of colonialism and done much to stimulate the guilty conscience of the rest of the European races. The Communist doctrine even encourages countries which have never been subject to colonial rule, such as Iran and Thailand, or have long since escaped from it, such as Greece or Brazil, to think of themselves as 'dependent territories'. The formerly oppressed peoples are the beneficiaries of both parts of this conjunction of circumstances. The question is, how long can it last?

It is also clear as a matter of history that the present scale of aid to under-developed countries is a by-product of the Cold War. On the western side at least, an important motive has been the fear that if the new and poor countries are not helped economically by the rich western nations they will 'go Communist'. The fear was ironically expressed in the story of an Asian prime minister, seeking a large loan from the US government, who was asked by Mr Dulles what his country had that would justify an American loan, and replied: 'Mr Secretary of State, my country has Communists.'

On the other side, the Soviet Union has certainly used foreign aid as a political weapon in the Cold War, so that many countries—India in particular—have been the beneficiaries from both sides. The question is whether the benefits would continue if the tension between the major powers were to be decisively relaxed. Many well-meaning people assume that such a relaxation ought to lead to even greater economic benefits for the poorer countries, because the rich would have more resources available for foreign aid; but they might well be mistaken, for several reasons. Not the least of them is that even in a partly disarmed world, security may be extremely expensive to maintain.

Another reason is that to some extent the resources available for foreign aid and those applied to the Cold War are complementary. It would not be a straightforward case of beating swords into ploughshares or converting nuclear weapons into tins of food and milk for starving Africans, as some well-meaning philanthropists have supposed. Foreign aid is given out of the surplus on the wealthier countries' balance of payments; that surplus is acquired, so far as Britain at least is concerned, largely by the strength and profitability of the science-based industries; and those industries are themselves closely linked with the defence programme.

This is not to say that Britain makes her living exclusively by exporting military aircraft and nuclear weapons, which would be immoral as well as untrue. But it is to say firstly that the export of the civil products of the aviation and electronics industries is highly profitable and likely to become more so; and secondly that military and civil programmes are necessarily so closely inter-related that without the defence stimulus those industries would be less advanced and less lucrative in the civil field as well.

In other words, the balance of payments would suffer from their decline, and the availability of foreign aid might be reduced. This is not a Machiavellian argument for maintaining a costly defence Budget for its own sake, but an indication of one of the consequences that has to be considered before cutting it to the bone.

A further reason is that, without the stimulus of fear and ideological competition, the inducement to aid under-developed countries might vanish. Those countries are sometimes unkindly described as parasites on the Cold War. Although the description may be just, it cannot be said for certain what would happen to their receipts of economic aid if the Cold War no longer prevailed.

On the whole, I incline to the belief that the consequences for them would not be so severe as is sometimes feared. Foreign aid was certainly stimulated to a considerable growth by the Cold War, but it began (at least in the British case) at an earlier date, and it seems now to have acquired a self-propelling momentum of its own. It would have been a fallacy to argue in 1950 that because the Welfare State in Britain was the outcome of a world war and a Socialist government, therefore it would be abolished when the war was forgotten under a Conservative government.

There is an element of the same fallacy in the belief that economic aid to under-developed countries would not outlive the Cold War. Nevertheless, the fact is that there is already a growing inclination, especially in the USA, to scrutinise foreign aid with a cold commercial eye. It will continue as long and as much as it is needed; but the prudent assumption is that that will not be for ever.

A number of considerations therefore suggest that the present relation between the old and the new states cannot be permanent. Both its material and its psychological foundations are bound to shift. Guilty consciences do not last for ever: the British people have already lost theirs over Ireland, for instance, though some Irishmen still think that we ought to go on paying for the wrongs done by Oliver Cromwell and the Black-and-Tans for a long time yet. Other principles begin to replace the shame of ancestral exploitation. One is that blood is thicker than water: so, for instance, Europeans in Africa doubt that the British people will continue indefinitely to act on the assumption that black Rhodesians must be right and white Rhodesians must be wrong.

From the point of view of the beneficiaries, too, the current assumptions seem bound to change in the long run. To be under-developed cannot be a permanent condition, and 'emergent' is clearly a transitional adjective. Poor countries are by no means necessarily poor in natural resources, and their populations are no longer to be regarded as naturally inferior to those of the former colonial powers—that is another part of the accepted dogma of our times.

There are good reasons then to regard the present situation as temporary. The new nations have come to stay: that is a simple fact which neither we nor they have yet sufficiently taken in. They are still enjoying the honeymoon period of independence, in which neither party to the new relationship can quite believe in it as permanent. To be accepted as a permanent and normal part of the international scene implies adherence to the reciprocal system of rights and obligations between equals which used to be known as the concert of nations. But so far as the new nations are concerned, the concert is not yet a symmetrical relation; and no one yet expects that it should be.

Thus the free press of Ghana can say what it likes about colonialist exploitation, but if the free press of Britain or the USA reports equally painful observations about Ghana their journalists are expelled; and no one expects it to be otherwise. Similarly, when India or Indonesia resorts to armed action against the Portuguese or the Dutch, or when the Algerian government expropriates French property in contravention of the independence agreements, no one expects it to be otherwise; and voices are even raised in Europe and America to approve these courses, or at least to justify them. Such a relationship is unequal and unhealthy, and it cannot be expected to last indefinitely.

It is, however, a perfectly natural phenomenon, and historically perhaps inevitable. The new nations are not to be blamed for taking advantage of the international situation in which they find themselves: the advantages, being inherent in the situation, are thrust upon them. The essence of the present situation, looked at in a long-term perspective, is that the new nations are going through exactly the same cycle of development as their seniors, the traditional states; but they are doing so out of phase with the traditional states and at a very different speed. The key to the long-term prospect is that eventually the two processes must move into phase and approximate to the same speed. This will entail adjustment on both sides.

There are basically three phases in the cycle of development, so far as we are familiar with it, since the emergence of the nation-state as the common unit of sovereignty. The first is the phase of nationalism, in which the most important attribute to acquire is sovereign independence within recognised geographical boundaries. It is essentially a selfish, or at any rate a self-regarding, phase: whatever lies within the magic circle of the nation is admirable, whatever lies outside it is suspect; though that does not preclude collaboration, for selfish ends, with other peoples whose nationalism happens to be compatible.

The second phase is that of inter-dependence, which comes with the discovery that first peace, and then prosperity, are indivisible. This is the phase of collective security and customs unions: enlightened self-interest replaces pure selfishness as the criterion, but the integrity of the nation-state is still sacrosanct in theory; patriotism is found to be not enough, but equally it is not superseded or condemned as obsolete.

The third phase is the most difficult to define, because

even the most mature states are only on the threshold of it. It is the phase in which peoples and governments come to recognise that the scope of human responsibility is not limited by national boundaries; and that it is both right and expedient to be willing to consider the subordination of national interests to the interests of humanity. 'No man is an Island, entire of itself', as Donne said; nor is any country, not even an island.

It is in this third phase that it becomes apparent that the nation-state is no longer by itself an adequate framework—as it once was, and as indeed the city-state once was before it—within which all the reasonable aspirations of its inhabitants, material and moral, can be satisfied. Once this is realised, the quest for a new international system begins, but very unevenly and uncertainly, because old habits of thought die hard and charity, which begins at home, is not easily extended to foreigners. Nevertheless the obsolescence, for many purposes, of national boundaries is a fact of international life to-day which cannot be ignored. The third phase is already before us.

The problem to which the following chapters are addressed is that there is a disequilibrium in the world to-day between countries which are going through different phases but which nevertheless have to co-exist in the same world. Different parts of the world have been out of phase in their development before, as for instance Europe, Asia and America were in the 15th century or Britain and Japan in the 18th; but as there was then no significant contact between them it did not matter. To-day it matters very much that the advanced western countries are moving into the third phase while most of Asia and Latin America is in the second and most of Africa in the first.

The matter is complicated by the fact that the phases

are not water-tight. No people advances collectively over-night from the first to the second, or from the second to the third, shedding all traces of the old Adam on the way. The same country—France, for instance—can pro-duce in the same generation a prophet of international responsibility and an arch-priest of tradional nationalism.

Clear enough distinctions can be drawn, however, to show the disequilibrium in which the world at present lives and the gaps that have to be closed before a new concert of nations can emerge. I shall try to explain the nature and origins of the disequilibrium without passing moral judgments on anyone for behaving in ways which were probably unavoidable in any case. But if blame is to be imputed at all it should be imputed first and fore-most to the philosophical Frankensteins of the 18th century, who invented the doctrine of nationalism and let it loose on an innocent and unsuspecting world.

2

The Old Nationalism

NATIONALISM was invented in Europe less than two hundred years ago and has since spread all over the world. It has undergone radical changes of character and content since the 18th century, both in its European setting and in the rest of the world, so that almost the only persistent feature of the doctrine from beginning to end is the strong collective emotion which it inspires. Originally and essentially, it is the doctrine that mankind is naturally divided into nations and that these constitute the natural units of political sovereignty. Nature has decreed, so it is believed, that nations and states should be co-terminous. The allegedly natural and self-evident character of these propositions is essential to them.

There were of course nations before there were nation-states. Medieval universities were divided into 'nations', which were fundamentally linguistic divisions. Shakespeare, to whom we owe perhaps the first of the long series of anecdotes involving an Englishman, a Scotsman, a Welshman and an Irishman, has the last of the four plaintively asking: 'What is my nation?'—a question which no one can answer. Hume wrote an essay, *Of National Characters*, in which again the word 'nation' is used as a collective noun, though with no specially political connotation.

Originally it meant simply a group into which one was born, having presumably (though this is not explicit in the etymology) common affinities of some kind, especially race, religion and language. It was left to the 18th- and 19th-century theorists—French encyclopaedists, German metaphysicians and English poets—to discover that these characteristics also ought to, and therefore do, define the bounds of political sovereignty.

The facts have never fitted the theory exactly, even in the most promising cases. There have always been nations which are divided between several states, as the Germans and Italians were when the theory was invented (and the Germans are again to-day). There have also been states which included several nations, such as the Ottoman Empire, the Austro-Hungarian Empire and the Swiss Republic.

Great Britain, with its three nations (or four if the Irish were included), has been another example. If the British are considered to be collectively a nation in themselves, then they were also an example of the other anomaly in the heyday of nationalism, since the British colonists had already established a separate sovereignty in America, thus dividing the British nation. All such anomalies were anathema to the theorists of nationalism, who set about rectifying them in Europe by re-drawing the boundaries of states to conform with nationality.

The boundaries could only be re-drawn by force, and the desire to do so was attractive not only to oppressed minorities but to conquerors with megalomaniac ambitions like Napoleon and Hitler. Napoleon appealed to the nationalist appetites of the Italians, the Greeks, the Hungarians, the Poles as instruments in his wars of conquest against the Austro-Hungarian and Russian Empires. Hitler made similar appeals with even more unscrupulous cynicism. Hardly less damaging were the pacific, high-minded but essentially muddle-headed interventions of the university teacher who was successively President of Princeton University and of the United States of America, Woodrow Wilson.

The effect of all this re-drawing of the map of Europe

over a period of a century and a half was merely to shift the burden to and fro between the shoulders of different minorities. Before the First World War, for instance, the Polish nation was divided between two multi-national empires; after it, the nation-state of Poland included (on official figures, which do not exaggerate in these cases) a one-third minority composed of Ukrainians, Russians, Germans, Jews and others.

Such costly absurdities arose from the sheer impossibility of defining a nation with precision at the margin. In the classic area of Macedonia, which has given the French language its word for 'fruit-salad',* it is possible by linguistic tests to allocate the same territory to the Greek, Bulgarian and Serb nationalities. The reason is that, quite apart from the ethnic intermixture within each village or valley, the same people may answer the questions put to them in a different language and a different sense according to the nationality of the questioner.

It is even possible to claim—and it has been claimed—the existence of a Macedonian nation-state, with a language of its own. The case for Macedonia might seem no worse than that for Albania, with its three religions and at least four ethnic and linguistic divisions, shared by a population of about one million. But in practice national frontiers are settled and maintained by the old-fashioned arbitrament of power, not by metaphysical doctrines.

In retrospect it may seem difficult to see why nationalist theory missed such elementary facts. The notion that Europe could be taken to pieces at the seams, so as to fall apart into self-contained national units, was always self-contradictory, since nationalist theory required that each nation should seek to include within its geographical

* *Macédoine*—defined by the Oxford Dictionary as a dish of diced fruit or vegetables in jelly.

boundaries every individual of its own nationality, regardless of the number of foreign minorities which must thereby be included as well. Nationalism thus led automatically to war—not only to wars of liberation against foreign oppressors, but also to consequential wars of irredentism against other ex-minorities.

Yet the philosophers of nationalism associated their theory with all that was most desirable: independence, peace and stability in international relations; democracy, liberalism and justice at home. These were the external and internal facets of nationalism respectively as seen by its theoretical exponents. But what nationalism in fact led to in Europe was domestic tyranny and aggressive imperialism.

To be fair, not every political theorist was so deceived. Two contrasted quotations from thoughtful British writers of the 19th century will serve to define the two poles between which political ideas have moved. John Stuart Mill wrote in his *Considerations on Representative Government*: 'It is, in general, a necessary condition of free institutions that the boundaries of government should coincide in the main with those of nationality.' On the other hand, Lord Acton wrote in his essay on *Nationality*: 'If we take the establishment of liberty for the realization of moral duties to be the end of civil society, we must conclude that those states are the most perfect which, like the British and Austrian Empires, include various distinct nationalities without oppressing them.... A state which is incompetent to satisfy different races condemns itself.'

Both were speaking of internal relations within a state, but both would also no doubt have expressed the same verdict if they had been considering external relations. In retrospect, Acton appears to show the greater wisdom, but certainly Mill more effectively represented the fashionable aspirations of his day and of the immediately following generations.

It is not hard to see how in fact the theorists of nationalism led themselves astray. From Kant to Woodrow Wilson, they were preoccupied with the idea of self-determination. The 'self' implied in that phrase was of course the individual man; but it was universally accepted—as indeed it had been by political theorists since Aristotle—that man could only fulfil himself as a member of society. Self-determination therefore implied both a relationship of freedom and equality between men within their society, and also a relationship between men collectively as members of societies.

The assumption was that by the act of self-determination men would not only choose the most natural relationship between themselves, which was democracy, but also the most natural organisation of their collective society, which was the nation. These two choices were contrasted with their antitheses which, although philosophically wrong, had hitherto prevailed—autocracies established by force, without popular consent, over peoples not of the same nation.

What the philosophers had not appreciated was the explosive character of the natural criteria by which they sought to define the nation: language, religion and race.

Language is clearly a sharp and potent discriminator, since nothing is easier than to promote suspicion and contempt of the foreign and the incomprehensible. The celebrated Greek saying that 'every non-Greek is a barbarian' is itself derived from a linguistic proposition, since etymologically a barbarian is merely one who talks gibberish. Every nation has the same feeling about its language, and nationalist philosophers have encouraged it. The 'fatherland of the German', according to the poet Arndt, who may be taken as typical, is 'as far as the

German tongue sounds ... where anger roots out foreign nonsense, where every Frenchman is called enemy ...' and so on.

Religion, on the other hand, though closely linked to language and once the bitterest of all sources of division, has become in the last hundred years a waning force in this context, at least in Europe. Its place has been taken by race, with its mysterious implications of purity in the blood on the one hand and sexual repugnance on the other.

The notion of racial superiority is the link between nationalism as a theory and aggressive imperialism in practice. It may not have been directly because Englishmen and Frenchmen thought themselves superior to Asians and Africans that they set out to conquer tropical territories, but it was certainly advanced as their moral justification for doing so. The empire-builders had many acknowledged motives. There were economic motives—to secure investments, to exploit natural resources, and to promote legitimate trade. There were missionary motives —to convert the heathen and abolish uncivilised practices like the slave trade or ritual murder.

There were the motives of strategic rivalry between the European nations, though usually the representatives of the imperial governments themselves were almost the last upon the colonial scene. There were the motives of adventurers and malcontents who wanted a new way of life, or sought like Clive and Raffles and Rhodes to extend national power for its own sake. From the point of view of the defeated Asians and Africans, these last formed the typical class of imperialists; and they also epitomised the latent assumption common to all, that of representing a race apart.

The defeated Asians and Africans, who had, after all, possessed a civilisation of their own which was not necessarily inferior to that of Europe a few hundred years earlier, naturally sought the key to the force that had overwhelmed them; nor did, nor could, the Europeans make any secret of it. Their superiority in all the practical arts of war and peace was manifest: in technology, science and industry, in medicine and education, in commercial, military and administrative techniques. All these bases of material improvement were introduced, consciously and unconsciously, into Asia and Africa for the first time—at any rate in the post-medieval era—by European administrators, traders, soldiers and missionaries.

Of course much that colonialism did was evil, and the balance of evil and good will never find an agreed settlement; but that is beside the point, for the evil and the good were inseparable. The point is that virtually every change, whether for good or ill, that was brought about in the way of life of the European colonies in Asia and Africa for the best part of a hundred years was the work of the colonial powers.

A further and more important point is that, once imperialism was launched, the process was inevitable. Frenchmen and Englishmen and the other imperial peoples could not have behaved otherwise than they did in their colonies without being untrue to themselves, with all their faults and merits. They were therefore bound to undermine the bases of their imperial power in the very course of consolidating it. They could not, even if they had wanted to, have prevented their subject peoples from acquiring the material arts and skills by which their empires had been won.

Nor could they have prevented them from deducing correctly that there was an ideological impulse behind the European conquest of the world, without which the material forces would have been as nugatory as were, for instance, the Chinese invention of gunpowder or the

26

Greek invention of steam-power. That ideological force could be identified without difficulty, by reading French and English books, by going to European universities, and by listening to colonial administrators' conversations, as the doctrine of nationalism. The Open Sesame was an open secret.

The secret was learned in different parts of the world at different times. There were large regions in which it scarcely needed learning, because the dominant populations were European by descent and represented simply an extension of European civilisation. Such were the whole of the Americas, north and south, whose struggles for national independence were virtually completed by the middle of the 19th century; and Australia, New Zealand and South Africa, which needed only half a century longer. These are not normally regarded as forming part of the history of the emergence of new nations, presumably because their nationalism is inseparable from that of the British, French, Dutch, Spanish and Portuguese from whom they derived.

The crucial moment came when nationalism began to emerge in territories where Europeans ruled alien races: in chronological order, first in the Middle East (including the Maghreb, or Arabic-speaking North Africa); then in Asia; then in Africa south of the Sahara; and finally in the scattered islands and other small territories all over the world, of which the largest concentration is in the Caribbean.

Before looking at these regions of 20th-century nationalism in turn, however, it is worth looking first briefly at Latin America, since it might reasonably be expected that the experience of the Latin American republics, most of which have been independent for more than a century, would hold lessons for the still newer world of Asia and Africa. Their experience has indeed served warning on the rest of the emergent states of the world, though it is not easy to see how the lessons could be applied. The basic lesson in the political context is that independence by itself is not enough.

After a century of emancipation, and after trying every system of government from democracy to absolute monarchy, with frequent excursions into military dictatorship, none of the Latin American countries has yet settled down with a stable form of constitutional government. Towards the end of the 1950s there was a marked trend back towards experiments in democracy, but the trend was sharply interrupted by the success of President Castro in Cuba—by far the most dynamic figure of the day in Latin American politics and the head of the only Communist régime in the western hemisphere.

Many latter-day nationalists would argue that the Latin American republics are not even truly independent because of their economic dependence on the USA. The lesson for the new Asian and African states, it would be argued, is that they must at all costs avoid the 'neo-colonialism' implicit in such dependence, to which a parallel can be found in the relationship established by the French with their ex-colonies in Africa.

There is clearly a good deal of truth in this argument. Many of the Latin American republics have to rely to an excessive degree in their foreign trade upon a single product. More than half, and in some cases as much as ninety per cent, of their export earnings are owed by Venezuela to oil; by Brazil, Colombia and El Salvador to coffee; by Cuba to sugar; by Chile to copper; by Bolivia to tin; by Ecuador, Honduras and Panama to bananas. Moreover, in most cases the USA is by far the largest single customer, though in the case of Cuba political differences have led to a drastic re-orientation of the trade.

There have been two major consequences of these economic facts. One is that the Latin American republics have come to be looked upon as virtually satellites of the USA, particularly in their voting at the United Nations, where for many years they formed (with the People's Democracies of Eastern Europe) one of the only two genuinely coherent *blocs*. The other consequence is that a strong resistance has grown up in Latin America to what is called 'dollar imperialism' (a phrase invented, curiously enough, by the US President Theodore Roosevelt), which takes a number of emotional forms. The physical attacks on Vice-President Nixon in his tour of Latin America in 1958 were one example, which greatly surprised and shocked the Americans. A sneaking sympathy for the outrageous conduct of President Castro is another manifestation. But the most persistent and damaging form which anti-Americanism takes is the capricious and generally hostile attitude of the Latin American republics towards foreign capital.

Economic nationalism is a strong force in Latin America, though not a very well-directed one. The need for foreign capital is indisputable: the mineral resources of the continent cannot possibly be exploited without it. But past experience has led most of the governments at one time or another to decide either to exclude foreign capital altogether, or to impose such restrictive conditions on it, or to pursue such unacceptable economic policies, as in effect to drive it away.

Nationalist sentiment applauds such economic suicide and deplores any deviation from it, The classic example was the fall of President Peron in Argentina, which was precipitated by his decision to bring in foreign capital and enterprise in 1955 to develop the country's oil resources. There is no readily apparent solution to the dilemma of choosing between continued poverty without foreign investment and the prospect of economic growth with foreign participation, which extreme nationalists condemn as 'neo-colonialism'.

There are however some lessons which can profitably be studied elsewhere. One is that in their desire to industrialise too rapidly—which is regarded as the hallmark of a truly independent power in the 20th century—the Latin American countries have neglected their agriculture and even discriminated against it. Wisely, President Castro has seen this mistake and has declared his intention to save Cuba from it. But it is a mistake widely committed elsewhere, from which the new African states in particular might well take warning.

Another lesson is that the collective economy of Latin America would be vastly stronger if it had not been broken up into a multiplicity of nation-states, or if some way could be devised of re-uniting them. In this way the problem, experienced by each country separately, of dependence on a single product would be overcome. It is significant that the best economic prospect in the long run is that of Brazil, which is by far the largest country in the continent. Brazil, in fact, is roughly co-terminous with the old Portuguese Empire in South America, whereas the rest of the independent states are the fragments of the former Spanish Empire.

A possible solution, in currently fashionable terms, would be the formation of a Latin American Common Market, and this idea has warm and skilful advocates. But it likewise runs counter to the strong tradition of economic nationalism. Historically there has in fact been relatively little trade between the Latin American states, whose exports generally go much farther afield, to Europe and the USA. Such manufacturing industry as they have is mainly for local consumption and the tendency in all of them is to try to make themselves more nearly self-supporting. Even those which were at one time major importers of foodstuffs, such as wheat and sugar, have steadily increased their own production in order to achieve self-sufficiency. The prospect of a common market for the whole region is therefore remote, although it might be more practical on a limited scale, for instance between some of the small Central American republics. Poor communications and intense nationalism are likely to be insuperable barriers between the great majority.

Like other ex-colonial peoples, the Latin Americans are inclined to blame their troubles, and even their internecine feuds, on the fact that imperialism has not yet been finally liquidated in the region. There is some truth in the complaint. American interests are not confined to investments: there is also a strategic interest in the Panama Canal, and an intense anxiety caused by the proximity of a Communist government in Cuba, with a consequential threat to the security of other Caribbean territories.

Britain, France and the Netherlands still have colonies in the region also. The British government tried sincerely to create a viable substitute for its colonial régime in the Caribbean by creating a Federation of the West Indies, but with small success. In other cases solutions are even harder to find; and for once the U S government is not in a hurry to force out the colonial powers, especially when it foresees the possibility that the first independent government of Guiana might be Communist.

There is therefore something of a case for arguing that imperialism is not played out in Latin America, but it is a gross exaggeration to attribute the woes of the region to its survival. Many Latin American states recognise the absurdity of it. Argentina and Chile, for instance, which both have territorial claims against Britain in the

Falkland Islands, pursue them with a sophisticated lack of bitterness and even with good humour; only the claim of Guatemala upon British Honduras generates even a show of bitterness. On the whole, the anxiety of the former colonial powers to liquidate their commitments is probably stronger than the anxiety of the Latin Americans to be rid of them. Things might well be worse, in some ways, without them. The grievance has a psychological value of its own; but, as elsewhere, it will not be there for ever.

Perhaps the outstanding lesson of the Latin American experience is not one for the other regions of emergent nationalism so much as for the rest of the world. It is that a very long time is likely to elapse before the nationalist revolution is played out.

European theorists believed in the 19th century that national independence was the sovereign cure for all political troubles, and self-determination the supreme political good. European experience has not borne out this belief, though some encouragement for it might be derived from the experience of purely European peoples overseas—Canada, Australia, New Zealand, the USA— where the essential condition was that they were safely removed from the practitioners of any rival nationalism. Latin America, although organically linked with European civilisation, certainly adds no credibility to the optimistic view. A century and a half after its nationalist revolution began, there is no sign of stability in sight.

It is prudent to remember this warning when examining the more recent nationalist revolutions of the Middle East, Asia and Africa.

3
The New Nationalism

IT IS EASY to see why the process of nationalist revolution was bound to be painful in the Middle East, Asia and Africa, simply by looking at the basic differentiae of nationalism: language, religion and race. There is a distinction between them, in that the first two are exportable, but the third is not. Europeans could, and did, induce Asians and Africans to adopt European languages and the Christian religion. In the case of language they were generally successful everywhere and with little resistance, so that French and English are now the languages of higher education and administration in many parts of Africa and Asia.

With the European forms of the Christian religion they were less completely successful, since there was stronger indigenous resistance—particularly in Asia, which is, after all, the breeding-ground of every major religion in the history of the world. In the case of the third differentia, however, there could be no possibility of transmission at all. Asians and Africans could not become ethnically Europeans. They could only note that there seemed to be such a thing as racial superiority, and bide their time.

Their time came in different ways, and not simultaneously. It is easy to see why it came first in the Middle East, because there the ruling power—the Ottoman Empire—was overthrown by the First World War, whereas it was not until the Second World War that European imperialism was shaken in Asia and Africa. The collapse of the Ottoman Empire marked the first stage, but only the first, in the fruition of Arab nationalism; and Turkish nationalism, which had the unusual but clearly logical purpose of contracting the national boundaries to the national heart-land in Anatolia, also came to fruition consequently at the same time.

But this was not the beginning of the story in the Middle East. There was already an Iranian nation-state, with twenty-five centuries of more or less independent history within more or less the same boundaries. There was also an Egyptian nation-state, which had been created in the early 19th century but taken over intact by the British. Iran and Egypt, with Turkey and Israel, are the only states in the Middle East which have a sense of nationality of the European kind. Arab nationalism, on the other hand, is a thing apart.

The Arabs did not feel themselves to be a nation in the strictly European sense, with a single capital and a central government over a defined territory inside fixed frontiers. If they did so, the Arab nation-state would be vastly more extensive than any of the European models. On the other hand, they equally never imagined the Arab nation carved up into a dozen separate states and a dozen more petty sheikhdoms, as happened between the world wars. Consequently Arab nationalism pursued a peculiar course.

It began by being pro-French and pro-British, since France and Britain were the models and the inspiration of nationalism. But the friendliness turned to bitter antagonism when the Europeans frustrated the purpose for which the Arab revolt had been launched, by carving up the ex-Ottoman territories into separate states; when the French further sought to turn their Mandates (Syria and Lebanon) into colonies; and when above all the British helped to create a Jewish state in Palestine. A new nationalist struggle had to be waged to get rid of the

European powers; and even though it was largely success-ful, it was by then well-nigh impossible to re-unite the Arab nation by abolishing the inter-Arab frontiers.

It was impossible partly because the separate Arab states reached independence at different dates and with different, but equally entrenched, political systems; partly also for economic reasons. In most cases the politi-cal system which first emerged was monarchy, under families whose members had played leading parts in the first nationalist revolution. These families represented and maintained an old-fashioned social system; and they enjoyed close links with the western powers, which owed them a debt of loyalty for their resistance to the Ottoman Empire. By reaction, the next generation of nationalists, of whom President Nasser was the archetype, became anti-western, republican, and ardent social reformers.

As republics, however, they found Arab unity no easier to achieve than it had been under the rival monarchies. They had Kant's authority—a weighty one among all philosophical nationalists—for the view that only a system of republics could guarantee peace and stability. But Kantian republics were intended to be elective democracies, not autocracies in which power changed hands only by military *coups d'état*.

The only parliamentary democracy in the Middle East by European criteria is Israel, which is looked upon by the Arabs as a European enclave established by force in their midst. In the Arab world, a republic is no more a democracy than was a hereditary monarchy. Con-sequently, despite many attempts at union, the two lead-ing Arab states, Egypt and Iraq, found themselves just as bitter rivals under their presidents as they had been under their monarchs. For this rivalry there is also an economic reason as well as reasons of political history: it is simply that Egypt is poor and Iraq is rich.

The economic consequences of the first nationalist revolution in the Middle East were unforeseen by its European instigators as well as by its Arab victims. Part of the consequences could not have been foreseen at all. The economies of Middle Eastern countries can be divided under two heads: those that depend on oil, and the rest. By the same criterion, the countries divide themselves into the rich and the poor. Since a full Arab union would involve a sharing of the wealth of the rich with the poor, there are strong economic incentives for the rich to seek to preserve the national boundaries created for them by the western powers.

Pressure for a pan-Arab political union thus tends to come from the states which have no oil—Egypt, Syria, Yemen, for instance—and to be resisted by those which have oil—Iraq, Saudi Arabia, Kuweit and the luckier sheikhdoms of the Persian Gulf. In the latter countries Arab nationalism among the middle classes is no less strong than in the former, and takes the particular form of hero-worshipping President Nasser; but it becomes in practice less enthusiastic as they attain or approach nearer to political power.

There are also factors in other sectors of the national economies of the Middle East which tend to preserve the present artificial boundaries. Apart from oil, Arab countries produce much the same sort of goods: cotton, tobacco, fruits and other agricultural and animal products. Their economies are therefore competitive, not complementary, and they trade very little with each other. In this respect they resemble the Latin American countries, where also economic nationalism is very strong.

Political lip-service is paid to the theory of blood-brotherhood, based on cultural, religious and racial affinity. But the merchants and entrepreneurs of the

Middle East have little desire to see the disappearance of the national boundaries which protect them from their economic rivals. Consequently there are grounds for seeking to preserve the *status quo* while talking passionately of Arab unity and blaming the western powers for frustrating it. Arab nationalism as an emotional reservoir will always remain stimulating and inexhaustible, but conceived as a political reality, stretching from the Atlantic Ocean to the Persian Gulf, it is more likely to prove a mirage.

The purposes for which nationalist emotion can be tapped vary throughout the region to an extent which is bewildering to European observers, and they do so not only in the Arab world but among the other peoples of the Middle East as well. What is particularly striking is the way in which the emotion can be tapped not only to excite hostility against foreigners but also for internecine purposes amounting virtually to civil war. It was, for instance, nationalism which brought Musaddiq to power in Iran in 1951, but it was also nationalism which brought him down in 1953; and President Kassim of Iraq went through exactly the same cycle between 1958 and 1962.

Every revolution in Syria since independence, which means roughly once every two years on average since the Second World War, has been a nationalist revolution. The republican rising in the Yemen in 1962 was nationalist in inspiration; and so was the royalist reaction to it. It was nationalism, mobilised by President Nasser against the British, which caused the dismissal of General Glubb from the Arab Legion by the King of Jordan; and nationalism, mobilised by the King of Jordan against the adherents of President Nasser, which saved Jordan from disintegration and partition a few years later.

The one constant factor in all these disturbances is that none of them in the event altered the geographical boundaries of the Middle East states in the smallest degree. All of them took place within existing national boundaries, artificial though these boundaries may be considered to be.

Perhaps the most instructive illustration of the way in which nationalism is beginning to be insulated and contained is one that lies only marginally within the Middle East: the Cyprus dispute in the 1950s. Here Greek nationalism played the role that is more familiar in the case of Arab nationalism. What the Greek Cypriots wanted was not independence nor even self-government, but amalgamation with the Greek nation-state: the term used was *Enosis*, which means 'union'. The violence which they perpetrated in the name of nationalism might, if it had occurred a generation or two earlier, or even if it had been more carefully controlled in the 1950s, have produced the result they desired. As things were, however, it served only to spark off the latent nationalism of the Turkish minority in Cyprus, supported by the Turks of the mainland, who had hitherto disinterested themselves in the island for a generation.

Characteristically, too, the majority of the victims of Greek nationalist frenzy were other Greeks. The upshot, after five years of bloodshed, was that Cyprus was left intact within its own island boundaries as a nominally independent bi-racial republic, a compromise which does not completely satisfy anyone but which even the renewed violence at the end of 1963 failed to destroy completely. If this case contains any general lesson, it is that the historic trend is now towards stability and the minimum tolerable change.

If this general inference is correct, then the broad pattern of existing nation-states (Turkey, Iran, Israel and perhaps Egypt) and pseudo-nation-states (the Arabic-speaking countries) is likely to survive more or less intact. But modifications of it are bound to continue to be sought. Public attention is attracted mostly by the major upheavals: the efforts to destroy Israel or Jordan, for instance, and the attempts to form federal unions, both in the Middle East proper and in the Maghreb.

Even more intractable problems, however, exist on a minor scale and in less conspicuous forms. One is that minorities remain embedded in the Middle East, divided between the nation-states, which have an equal right to call themselves nations by the philosophical rules of nationalism: the Kurds, the Armenians and the Berbers, for instance. Their problems used to be much more satisfactorily soluble, in principle at any rate, within the *millet*-system of the Ottoman Empire; but to-day they are from their own point of view victims of oppression, and from the established government's point of view a source of disruption and subversion.

Another unsolved problem is, in a sense, the exact converse: it is the survival of sovereign units of minuscule size, particularly round the eastern and southern shores of the Arabian peninsula, which cannot be considered nation-states in the ordinary sense and yet cannot be peacefully disposed of in any obvious way. Economic and political logic suggests that they should be grouped in federations, as has been attempted among the Aden Protectorates and might be with some of the Persian Gulf sheikhdoms. But the particularism of petty potentates is hard to overcome, especially when all of them hope to find oil under their deserts, as some have already done; and the danger of forcible absorption by larger states is serious.

Although it is apparent that the main targets of nationalist jealousies and hostilities to-day lie within the region itself, and almost every man sees his most dangerous enemy in his next-door neighbour, it would be wrong to suggest that this is the whole of the story. The nationalist revolution against the former imperial powers has by no means fully run its course, nor will it do so while the relics of imperialism still remain. The oldest British colony in the Middle East, Aden, is still a colony and still a source of contention with the Yemen, whether under republican or monarchical rule. The special relations by treaty between Britain and the sheikhs of the Persian Gulf are also resented, particularly by Saudi Arabia, which is the principal land-neighbour of all of them.

In the case of Kuwait there is the same resentment on the part of the Iraqi republic, which has not been diminished by Kuwait's full independence; nor can the British interest there readily be liquidated, remembering that Kuwait produces a vast proportion of all Sterling Area oil and that the Kuwait Development Board is the largest single investor on the London Stock Exchange.

The principal reason for the maintenance of the few small remaining British footholds in the Middle East is of course oil, but there are also strategic reasons for them. Geography and geology have altered as the grounds for British interest in the area. What mattered first was where the Middle East lay on the map (on the route to India); then what lay under its barren deserts (oil); and now again its position on the map, straddling the air routes to the Far East and Australasia. Cyprus, Aden and a few small islands in the Indian Ocean are still essential staging-posts for the RAF. The internal stability and peace of the region are a serious concern of the British government.

Although no one any longer contemplates an attempt

to defend the Middle East from external attack by means of a large British force established in the area, as was done in the First and Second World Wars and was still contemplated so long as the Suez Canal Zone base existed, it has been thought necessary even more recently to create a defensive alliance for the area, the Central Treaty Organisation (CENTO), in which Britain is a member.

The US government shares these British interests in some degree: the USA is also virtually a full member of CENTO, and has Air Force bases in the heart of the Middle East. It is perhaps fair to say that the US interest in the Middle East is rather as one sector in a global system of defence strategy, and that oil is for the USA (being itself a very large oil-producer) a relatively secondary interest.

Whatever the motives, however, the resentment of the visible presence of the western powers in the area is none the less strong. It is unlikely to diminish so long as that presence remains. The form of the presence is less offensive and more tactfully managed than in the past, but even so its days may be numbered. CENTO served a useful purpose in its early days, particularly in stabilising Iran against subversion, but it has been seriously questioned in recent years whether it might not be regarded as expendable. The British relation with the sheikhdoms of the Persian Gulf is also looked on by many as an anachronism, as indeed they are themselves.

Inevitably the association of Britain with such old-fashioned manifestations of a bygone age is regarded as an affront by Arab nationalists, not only because it has a lingering savour of imperialism but because nationalism is preoccupied just as much with modernisation and social reform as with independence. The attraction of President Nasser to Arab nationalists is that these are the things he stands for, whether or not he actually achieves them in Egypt; and Egyptian propaganda, through films, broadcasting, television, newspapers, books and school-teachers, is highly effective among millions of Arabs who have never seen Egypt. (The closer neighbours of Egypt, however, such as the Sudan, Libya and Tunisia, are less enthusiastic admirers of President Nasser.)

Britain, on the other hand, still seems to be linked with the past which the new Arab intelligentsia is trying to escape from, even though in practical terms Britain and her friends stand for a more efficient and orderly way of doing things. In this conflict the spirit that is at present embodied in Nasserism (whatever the personal fate of President Nasser) seems likely to prevail in the end.

Two factors have been deliberately omitted from the foregoing account of the consequences of independence in the Middle East: religion and Communism. Contrary to much popular theorising, neither has played a serious part in the history of Middle Eastern nationalism, which has been essentially secular and patriotic in its inspiration.

The Muhammadan religion is a potent vehicle of emotion, which has often been stirred up by nationalists in their revolutionary phases, but sooner or later religious fanaticism has proved to be a tiresome rival of nationalism, which the secular rulers have had to put down; and they have generally succeeded in doing so without too much difficulty. The bitter division of Islam between the Sunni and Shiite sects, not to mention the smaller heresies, also militates against it as a political force. Almost the only permanent political consequence of a religious origin is the separation of the Lebanon, with its predominantly Christian population, from Syria.

Communism as a creed has also been no more than an irritant in the nationalist politics of the Middle East, though of course the political influence of the Soviet

Union—the nearest of all the great powers to the area—is quite another matter. It was the proximity of the Soviet Union, not any special attributes of Communism, that made the Tudeh Party so serious a menace for a time in Iran. At a further remove from the Soviet periphery—in Iraq, Syria and even in Cyprus—the fear that the Communists were about to usurp power has frequently been expressed; but there has never yet proved to be any reality in the fear, and it has always been grossly exaggerated by those whom it suited politically to do so.

Experience suggests it is in fact unlikely that a Communist régime could last long—at any rate without profoundly changing its character in a nationalist direction—in any country not readily accessible to the Red Army: in other words, unless it is within or in the immediate neighbourhood of the existing Soviet Empire. So long as Turkey and Iran remain free of it, Communism is unlikely to dominate the rest of the Middle East.

* * *

Although both religion and Communism can be largely left out of account in the evolution of the nation-state in the Middle East, it is quite otherwise in the rest of Asia. One major state in Asia owes its creation entirely to a religious dynamic—Pakistan; and another owes its existence and strength entirely to Communism—the People's Republic of China. Both are startlingly different from the European model of a nation-state.

China is vastly larger than any European state: its population is at least double that of the whole of non-Communist Europe combined; and it has a mass of languages which cannot inter-communicate except in their written form. Pakistan flouts all the rules of nationalism except the religious criterion: it has no *lingua franca* (except English among the educated classes), but two dominant languages and a mass of minority dialects; it is divided into two separate parts by a thousand miles of foreign territory; and on purely ethnic ground it would have no claim to a separate existence at all.

These examples merely illustrate the distinctiveness of Asia's experience. The modern history of Asia, like that of the Middle East, begins with the impact of the West and the reaction against that impact; and nationalism again provided the ideological impulse behind both the action and the reaction. But the impact was much more diverse and variegated in its origins, and so was the material on which it impinged. China, for instance, was penetrated (though never conquered) by half a dozen western powers, including Russia and the USA; Japan of her own volition took half-a-dozen different western models. South-East Asia (except Thailand, the elegant mistress of neutrality) was carved up between Britain, France, the Netherlands, Portugal and the USA.

Moreover, many Asian countries suffered imperialist aggression at the hands of other Asian countries. Japan once occupied Korea, Manchuria and South-East Asia; Communist China has occupied Tibet, infringed the territory of India, and promoted rebellion in Malaya and Vietnam. The Overseas Chinese remain as a permanent and dreaded fifth column throughout South-East Asia. Indians too have a large and vigorous *émigré* population, though no one suspects India of imperialism.

The Indian experience has been in every way unique. Having had only one imperial master, apart from residual French and Portuguese enclaves, and having made unexampled efforts to reconcile the British and Hindu genius, India emerged almost overnight in 1947 as one of the great states of the world. The only functioning democracy in Asia, the largest parliamentary democracy in the world, the possessor of a western-style civil service, legal system and armed forces, under British-educated leaders of the highest calibre—India was a unique phenomenon in Asia. The fusion of western and Asian nationalism was here seen at its best; but India is not, of course, a nation-state in the European sense, but rather a multi-national union like the Austro-Hungarian Empire.

It is a commonplace that the question whether the Indian or the Chinese system will be the more successful in solving the problems common to them both—over-population, under-development, poverty, illiteracy, technical backwardness—is crucial for the future of Asia and the world. But the prestige of both has lately suffered setbacks in the eyes of the world.

Clearly the nationalist revolution in Asia is not yet complete or stabilised. For this the fundamental reason is the overwhelming character of the economic problem, which distracts the best energies from the task of nation-building. In India and Pakistan certainly, in China presumably, the population consisting mainly of peasants is growing steadily at a faster rate than the available resources, including food. The national income *per caput* is therefore generally steady at a low level, or actually falling. This is the first and greatest problem of survival.

But there are also other problems of a political character which stand in the way of the new Asian states, and bulk even larger in the eyes of world opinion, particularly since they are constantly aired in public at the United Nations. They can be summed up under four heads: the relics of imperialism; the relics of the Second World War; the revival of pre-colonial rivalries; and the problem of plural societies and minorities.

The relics of imperialism consist of a number of small European enclaves in the immediate vicinity of the new

nation states, Hong Kong and Macao, Okinawa, Mauritius
and other islands in the Indian Ocean, Timor and so on.
Many have recently been disposed of: the French enclaves
in India by cession, the Portuguese by conquest; West
Irian to Indonesia under the threat of force; Singapore,
North Borneo and Sarawak by merger in the Federation
of Malaysia; but several of the most difficult still remain.
Secondly, the relics of the war are even more intractable.
They consist of the divided countries of Korea and Vietnam, and the island of Formosa split from China under
what is in effect a separate sovereign state.

Thirdly, the revival of pre-colonial rivalries is common
to every new Asian state, since there is none which has not
territorial claims against one or more of its neighbours,
too numerous to list in detail: the most serious being
those which have caused war between China and India,
and near-war between India and Pakistan.

Besides the territorial vestiges of the colonial period,
there is another ground for the Asians to argue that the
age of imperialism is not yet finished. It lies in the South-
East Asia Treaty Organisation, more of whose eight
members are western (the USA, Australia, New Zealand, Britain, France) than Asian (Pakistan, Thailand,
the Philippines). The treaty, signed in the aftermath of
the French *débâcle* in Indo-China, can only be said to
represent the highest common factor of agreement then
attainable; and the factor was neither high nor satisfactory. India and Burma refused to join; Malaya showed
no wish to do so on becoming independent; Laos and
Cambodia were left in the peculiar position of not being
parties to the treaty but entitled to invoke its protection;
and the USA explicitly declared that it regarded its
adherence to the treaty as limited to the care of Communist aggression. South Vietnam, which was left in the
same position as Laos and Cambodia, has in fact been

defended against aggression from the north by the USA alone; and the treaty has been invoked only once, by Thailand in 1961.

It is possible that renewed evidence of Chinese aggressiveness—for instance, against India—may have encouraged the South-East Asian members to congratulate themselves on having acquired western guarantees, in particular from the USA; and undoubtedly any attempt to liquidate the organisation would lead some of the governments in the area to conclude that they were being written off as expendable.

But it is not easy to prove that the treaty has added much of significance to the stability of the region, to set in the balance against the argument with which it arms the enemies of the West, that the imperialist presence is still there. The Pakistanis in particular have been inclined to wonder what they gained by the treaty that was not to be had without it. For instance, although, it is true that they have had arms supplied from the West, it is also true that the neutral Indians have had them too.

The fourth of the residual problems, that of plural societies and minorities, is perhaps the most fundamental of all, not only because it has connections with each of the other problems, either as cause or as consequence, but also because it goes to the very root of the claim of the Asian states to be nations at all. There are indeed nations, and great nations, in Asia, but they are even farther from coinciding with the political boundaries of sovereignty than anywhere else in the world.

There are, for instance, many millions of Chinese outside China, and they form very large components in the population of Malaysia, Indonesia and Thailand. Ceylon has a large proportion of Indian population; Burma contains substantial minorities of Karens, Shans and others claiming local autonomy; India has the same

47

problem with the Nagas and other racial groups; Indonesia has absorbed islands with populations quite distinct from the Javanese; and so on. If Asia were to consist of nation-states constructed according to orthodox European criteria, their number would run into three figures and there would be a continuous state of frontier-warfare between them.

Not that any such thing is likely to happen, of course: the trend is all the other way. Although nationalism is the universally recognised name for the ideological impulse in Asia, there is no Asian country except Japan that a 19th-century European nationalist would accept as a nation-state. China and India are vastly larger and more variegated than the wildest imaginings of philosophical nationalism. Pakistan and Indonesia, both with much larger populations than any European nation-state, are geographically fragmented. Malaysia flouts all the conventional criteria of national homogeneity—language, religion, race and even geography.

The other ex-colonial states of South-East Asia are nearest to the European model, but they lack entirely the nationalist drive towards modernisation and self-assertion, except where it is supplied from outside by Communism. The possibility cannot be ruled out that several of these states, as well as Korea and Formosa, might eventually be absorbed into the Communist Chinese Empire, unless there were to be a new intervention from the West. But even Communism, however much modified by Chinese experience, is still a western ideology. Europe cannot escape time's revenges.

* * *

The pace of events in Asia was leisurely compared to Africa. In Africa there was the same impact of western imperialism and the same nationalist reaction to it, but the process was more universal, briefer, and more thorough. It was more universal in that there was not an acre of Africa that did not at some time pass under titular foreign control, even if in some cases—for instance, Liberia and Sierra Leone, where refuges were created for emancipated slaves—the foreign intention was wholly benevolent.

The whole process was also spectacularly brief, apart from the establishment of forts and trading stations along the coastal periphery from the 16th century onwards. It was briefest of all in Abyssinia, which was under Italian rule only from 1936 to 1941; but nowhere was it protracted. Even Nigeria, the largest state on the African continent, only came into being under that name in 1914. Despite this brevity, however, the process was exceedingly thorough, partly because it was universal throughout the continent and partly because it rested on a conception of the African for which there was no parallel in Asia or the Middle East.

The most painful fact of the colonial period for the Europeans to live down is that they regarded the African as little better than sub-human. This attitude was explicitly taken by the descendants of the Dutch colonists, who named themselves Afrikaners and the Africans Kaffirs (an Arabic term of contempt, meaning 'infidels'); and the same attitude was taken by implication by almost every other European except the missionaries.

A typical judgment was made by one of Cecil Rhodes's followers, that the magnificent ruins at Zimbabwe in Southern Rhodesia could not have been built by Africans because Africans were congenitally incapable of creative activity. The failure of Africans even to invent the wheel was constantly held against them. Obviously such attitudes could not be taken towards 'the natives'

49

in Asia or the Middle East. It came to seem natural to treat Africans in humiliating ways which went far beyond anything that was done to other colonial peoples.

The terrible misjudgment committed by the Europeans about the Africans is the more difficult to excuse or explain because it was totally irrational; and rationality has always been paraded as a specifically European attribute. There must in fact have been rational explanations to account for the undoubted fact of African backwardness when the first contact with Europeans took place, but no congenital inferiority of Africans should have been among them. The climate, the mosquito and tsetse-fly, and the endemic diseases which go with them, are part of the explanation. The relative lack of energy-resources of the kind which promoted the European industrial revolution was another factor, though one which is likely to be dramatically reversed once the hydro-electric potential of the continent's rivers and lakes is fully exploited.

But first and foremost among the factors which kept Africans backward was probably the lamentable prejudice which declared that they were backward. The fact that this prejudice could be speciously reinforced from the Bible, as it still is by Nationalist theologians in South Africa, makes it a matter for astonishment, as well as congratulation to the missionaries, that Africans ever adopted Christianity at all.

As a result of these unreasoning attitudes, several things took place in Africa which took place nowhere else. Africans were captured and bought and sold as slaves by Europeans. Admittedly, the Europeans were only following the age-old practice of the Arabs; admittedly, too, it was the Europeans who eventually abolished and destroyed the slave-trade; but the traumatic experience remains a living fact of history, and the fruits of it are still being gathered in the USA.

The Europeans also destroyed the undeveloped forms of religion and political organisation in Africa, which seemed to them too crude to be treated as elements of civilisation. They did this most effectively in areas which were climatically suited to European settlement, such as Algeria, Angola and Mozambique, Kenya, the Rhodesias and South Africa, thus creating another problem that was unique to Africa: the problem of an established population of land-owning Europeans who looked on Africa as their home. The dual process of exporting black slaves and importing white settlers laid up a store of problems for Africa which will never be exhausted, so far as human foresight can tell.

The upshot is that although nationalism in Africa is as strong and as bitter an emotion as anywhere, and equally derived in its philosophy and vocabulary from Europe, it has little to do with nationality according to the conventional criteria of Europe. European colonial powers carved up Africa on lines which suited their convenience; and although these have now become the boundaries of independent states which are acquiring a strength and cohesion of their own, they do not fulfil Mill's criterion of coinciding with those of nationality.

Practically no African state south of the Saraha has a single *lingua franca* of its own, apart from one or other of the European languages; and there is already a noticeable division between French-speaking Africans and English-speaking Africans—sometimes of the same race—which is reflected in the two concepts of *négritude* and the 'African personality'. The units which command personal loyalty are in general either narrower than the nation or much wider; and both can be felt simultaneously by the same person.

The narrower loyalty is to the tribe, which is in some cases virtually equivalent to a nation. But even in such cases, the tribe is generally absorbed into a more comprehensive state system—for instance, the Ashanti in Ghana, the Kikuyu in Kenya, the Baganda in Uganda, the Barotse in Northern Rhodesia; or it is divided between two or more separate states—for instance, the Bakongo on the River Congo or the Somalis in the Horn of Africa. Only in a relatively few cases, such as Nyasaland and Basutoland, do the tribal 'nation' and the state more or less coincide.

Moreover, it is the declared intention of many African governments to complete the destruction of tribal society, which the Europeans began, in order to bring the whole of their people into the modern world. The contrary policy of the Nationalist Afrikaner government in South Africa, which seeks to resurrect tribal society in the Bantustans as the logical culmination of *apartheid,* is one of the principal grounds for African hostility and suspicion towards it.

The wider loyalty of the African goes to the concept of 'Pan-Africanism', which has the universality characteristic of the reaction to be expected against the equal universality of the Europeans' contempt and humiliation of the Africans in the past.

Europeans generally find Pan-Africanism amorphous and difficult to define, but the reason for this is probably quite simple. Pan-Africanism is the comprehensive reaction to the whole complex of attitudes and conduct of Europeans towards Africa in the past, and it is amorphous and ill-defined because they were multifarious. It is a human example of Newton's law of action and reaction. Pan-Africanism asserts the dignity and special quality of the black man, because that is precisely what the Europeans denied. Pan-Africanism first came to Africa from the Caribbean area and the USA: this was, so to speak, the *ricochet* of the slave-trade. Pan-Africanism aims at the unification of Africa: this is the reaction against what is called the policy of 'Balkanisation' imputed to the colonial powers, though of course the latent premise that Africa was once a unity is fallacious.

Because there were many European attitudes to Africa, many different and even inconsistent attitudes can be comprehended under the general title of Pan-Africanism. To some extremists, it is an assertion of the racial superiority of the black man; and this is an acceptable and even welcome attitude to European racialists, because it provides a counterpart to white nationalism and a logical justification for *apartheid*. Such African extremists detest white liberals and 'multi-racial experiments' even more than they detest Dr Verwoerd or Sir Roy Welensky.

Others interpret the idea of Pan-Africanism in a generous sense, meeting the European liberal halfway. For these, an African does not have to be black: he is anyone, of whatever race, for whom Africa is his birth-place and his home, and this definition logically includes not only the Arabs of North Africa but even the Afrikaners of the South. In some former colonies of European settlement, such as Northern Rhodesia, the races have already begun to make their peace on the basis of such a principle.

In Southern Rhodesia, South Africa and the Portuguese territories the prospect of such an outcome is exceedingly remote. It needs to be said that the reason does not lie solely in the stubborn unwisdom of the policy of the European ruling minorities towards the African majorities. There is also the important consideration that what African nationalists are seeking there is not national independence in the sense in which it has been claimed in any other country in the world. 'One man, one vote' in these territories does not mean national independence for the Africans: it means substituting black supremacy for white supremacy.

53

As a matter of pure logic, on the other hand, *apartheid* carried to its logical conclusion in geographical partition would mean national independence: that is the theoretical justification of Dr Verwoerd's policy, though not of his practices. It is not possible to foresee any solution of the problem in these particular countries, but it is only fair to see the reality of the dilemma in which European natives of Africa are placed.

The suddenness of African emancipation has inevitably left a great deal uncertain and unsettled even in the wholly African states. Will the thirty-odd new states which have emerged since 1957 consolidate themselves within the artificial boundaries left behind by the Europeans? Or will they disintegrate into smaller units? Or will they coalesce into much larger units?

Many Europeans feared disintegration in the early stages, particularly in Ghana and Nigeria, but the governments of both countries took severe and effective measures to prevent it. Some Africans—particularly President Nkrumah of Ghana—openly advocated the formation of larger federations and eventually of a single United States of Africa. The constitution of Ghana, like that of Egypt, provides for the delegation of sovereignty in part to a larger union, and Nkrumah took steps towards such a union with Guinea in 1959 and with Mali in 1960. A series of Pan-African conferences debated these issues during the first five years of independence. So far, the outcome has been that the existing states within their ex-colonial boundaries, marginally adjusted here and there, seem on the whole likely to survive.

In the original circumstances of emancipation, this would have seemed an unlikely outcome. The colonial boundaries left many tribes divided between two or more states, and few states were ethnically or linguistically homogeneous. In the early days a few frontier adjust-

54

ments were successfully made, enabling, for instance, British Togoland to join Ghana, the British Cameroons to join Nigeria, and the British and Italian Somalilands to amalgamate as the Somali Republic.

In the next stage many attempts were made to amalgamate ex-colonies into larger federations: the Mali Federation, the Maghreb Federation, the East African Federation, and others. But so far none of these has become a political reality. A number of unsatisfied territorial claims therefore remain to bedevil intra-African politics: the claim of Morocco to absorb Mauretania, for instance, and that of Togo on Ghana, and of Somalia to the north-eastern region of Kenya. On the whole, the likeliest outcome still appears to be an uneasy maintenance of the *status quo*.

Once a state has come into being it soon develops a strongly built-in mechanism of self-preservation, as the Kingdom of Jordan in the Middle East has shown for the past generation. The very process of meeting in international conference to discuss changes tends to consolidate the *status quo*, as became particularly clear at the most ambitious of the Pan-African Conferences held in Addis Ababa in 1963, which seemed to put an end to President Nkrumah's scheme for a political union of Africa.

Membership of the United Nations has a like effect, since no government likes to abdicate its seat at New York in the interests of a political dream: only Syria has ever done so, and soon thought better of it. Modern communications and administrative techniques soon knit together people who had no ties in the past, and once these have been created they are not easily dismantled and reconstructed. Like the non-nation-states of the Middle East, the non-nation-states of Africa have almost certainly come to stay, held together by what is paradoxically called nationalism.

They are not yet so sure, however, that they have come to stay. Looked at from Europe, in their present phase, the new African states seem to be in an extreme degree self-conscious and hyper-sensitive. They wish to play their proper and fully independent part in the world, but they expect the world to treat their own problems as pre-eminently important. To get the Portuguese out of Angola and Mozambique, to transfer power in Southern Rhodesia from Europeans to Africans, to abolish the *apartheid* legislation in South Africa: these are what they consider to be absolutely first priorities not only for Africa but for the world.

At the same time they suspect that the offending Adam has by no means yet been whipped out of the European soul. The formation of the European Economic Community, for instance, is looked upon as a camouflage for the re-imposition of 'colonialism' on Africa in an economic guise; and the French atomic tests in the Sahara were seen as a typical display of European insolence towards the 'expendable' natives of Africa.

* * *

The nationalist upheaval in Africa is therefore still farther than in Asia or the Middle East from having settled down on terms of comity and equality with the older nation-states. Its convulsive progress has had, moreover, the effect of carrying one stage farther the development of the principles on which the international system now rests: it has, in fact, overthrown almost unnoticed one of the rules which had hitherto been carefully followed in the process of colonial emancipation.

When the European powers began to relinquish their colonies, they originally required two standard conditions of independence: that a new state should be economically viable at its accustomed standard of living and that it should be reasonably capable of defending itself again any likely enemy, if necessary with the help of an alliance with its former sovereign power. Throughout the emancipation of the Middle East and Asia these two conditions were more or less maintained. In Africa they have had to be abandoned.

The consequences are already being felt elsewhere. If states so poor, or small, or weak, or all three, as Rwanda and Burundi, Mauretania, Nyasaland and Somalia can be accepted as fully independent, where can the line be drawn at all? Cyprus and Malta are also now accepted; the disintegration of the West Indies Federation into a number of independent islands need no longer seem so deplorable as it once did; Western Samoa has become independent, with its 430 square miles of islands and a population of 100,000. The question is naturally asked, why not Mauritius, Fiji, the Persian Gulf states, Swaziland, Hong Kong?

It is difficult to see how the total membership of the United Nations can eventually be kept below 150, though many of the new additions will represent populations barely running into six figures. Small though they are, some will have at least as much right to claim to be 'nations' as Pakistan or Nigeria, though some will also, like Cyprus or Mauritius, reflect all the problems of a plural society in microcosm.

Although the revolution precipitated by the doctrine of nationalism 200 years ago has not yet run its course, it is now possible to foresee without much ambiguity what its final pattern will be. Having first given birth to about a score of nation-states in Europe, and as many again of European descent elsewhere, it will soon have finished drawing on the map of the world the boundaries of about 150 distinct political units. Well over half of them had no independent existence a generation ago, and well over half the remainder, though nominally independent, counted for nothing at that date in the concert of nations.

Compared with the traditional nation-states, most of the new ones do not strictly speaking comprise nations at all. Many of them are, by the same comparison, minute and one or two are enormously large. Almost all are poor, or at any rate under-developed; though one or two are disproportionately rich. All are intensely proud and sensitive. There is inevitably a marked disequilibrium in their relations with the older and maturer states of the world.

The question is, into what pattern will those relations eventually settle down?

4

The Dual Standard

IT IS CLEARLY impossible to generalise constructively about so large and various a class of countries and peoples as the new states comprise. What they have in common amounts to little more than the labels 'newly emergent' and 'under-developed', which describe respectively their political and economic status. Even that status has come about in different ways.

A generation ago, most of the countries in question were colonies of European powers; but others were already nominally independent before the Second World War, and were even members of the League of Nations— for instance, Iran, Thailand, Egypt, Iraq, Abyssinia and most of the Latin American republics.

Also, they vary between extreme limits both in size, from India to Burundi, and in potential or actual wealth from Kuwait to Haiti. But whatever the variety of their political history or material prospects, at least some common features can be picked out among them, however much qualification may be needed in their general application.

The common character of their public behaviour may be described, in its simplest form, as self-assertion, and the principal forum for it is the United Nations. There are a number of foolish myths current in some European countries on the subject, such as the myth of the so-called Afro-Asian *bloc*, which invariably votes unanimously for the Communist line at the UN and never pays its subscriptions. The facts bear no relation to the picture drawn.

But it would be equally wrong to ignore the fact that the United Nations has become a uniquely valuable forum for the self-assertion of the new and small nations, in sharp contrast with the original intention of the great powers which created it. The responsibility for allowing this to happen lies with the lack of foresight shown by the great powers themselves. By rendering the Security Council ineffective through deadlock, they allowed unintended powers to pass into the hands of the General Assembly, where the mere numbers of the new nations gave them the effective voice.

The self-assertion of the new states is not made, however, as British and Frenchmen are apt to think, exclusively at the expense of the great powers. I have pointed out already that they have at least as many grievances in their relations with each other, or even internally, as they have against the great powers. The United Nations has heard the Arab states doing battle ferociously with each other, the Latin Americans with Castro, India with Pakistan, Ghana with Togo. It has also heard the grievances of minorities within the new states, such as the Nagas in India and the Somalis in Kenya, and it will certainly hear more of these.

But there is a more important feature common to the conduct of the new nations which has to be recognised at this point. It is that they apply to themselves, and to each other, different standards of judgment from those which they apply to the great powers or to the ex-imperialist Europeans. The dual standard, which is at the root of what Lord Home called Britain's 'appalling dilemma' in a celebrated speech at the end of 1961, manifests itself in every relationship: in their own behaviour, in their judgments of others—particularly the rival great powers—and in their expectations from the rest of the world.

A common form taken by the self-assertiveness of many new states is that of quickly discarding, or radically altering, the political systems bequeathed to them by their former masters. The natural consequence is the formation of one-party governments as in India, Ghana and Algeria. It is natural because in the period of foreign rule there is only one political cause that matters, which is independence, so that all able and patriotic men and women tend to join a single organisation. Not to belong to the nationalist organisation is to display an unpatriotic attitude; to belong to a rival organisation representing a minority interest is to split the nationalist cause, which is treason. Consequently when independence is achieved, there is virtually no other party to belong to; or if there is, it is soon eliminated, perhaps on the grounds that it must have been covertly in league with the imperialists.

The alternative process, especially in countries which had no great struggle for liberation, like Ceylon, the West Indies, or the ex-Belgian Congo, is the formation of purely personal followings behind particular leaders. This carries the danger of promoting the disintegration of the state itself, as happened in the Federation of the West Indies and the Congo, and was perhaps only narrowly averted in Ghana and Nigeria by strong and questionable measures. The same danger, with the same consequential need for strong measures in order to preserve the state, has arisen in many cases from divisions on other lines of a non-political character. They may be the lines of race, or religion; or lines which combine the two.

Examples of racial divisions are common in Africa, where Asians and Europeans as well as Africans have to co-exist, and also in Asia, where Chinese, Indians and Malays, though all Asians in race, have no political sentiment in common; and even farther afield, there is the case of British Guiana, torn by the bitter rivalry of Africans and Indians. There are also many cases of religious division: a spectacular example is Southern Vietnam, where Buddhist leaders in 1963 resorted to voluntary martyrdom in protest against the political domination of the Christian minority. Of the third kind, where religion and race combine to divide a newly created state, the most clear-cut case is Cyprus, where the division of Turk and Greek nearly coincides with that of Muhammadan and Christian.

Countries divided along such lines are cruelly exposed to the danger of violence, and violence breeds repression. One way or another, either strong measures or the evolution of one-party rule contain the seeds of dictatorship. Dictatorship may indeed help to advance a country's stability and standing in the world, but it cannot avoid also being a threat to civil liberties and to many other things that western democracies value. In this case the criticism of a dual standard as between the new states and their seniors can unfortunately be answered by pointing to dictatorships in Europe too—for instance, Portugal and even France.

But the point is that liberal opinion does not defend dictatorships in Europe, and ought therefore to feel entitled to condemn dictatorial practices in Asia or Africa. It is not always inclined to do so; and that disinclination is, in fact, an example of the dual standard in operation.

The least excusable application of the dual standard is in the treatment of human rights by some of the new nations, in contrast to the behaviour they expect of the European powers. Examples are unfortunately very numerous, and can be found almost daily in reputable English newspapers which are normally sympathetic to the new nations. The methods used by President Nkrumah to curb the principal opposition party in Ghana and to restrict the constitutional rights of the Ashanti tribe are a widely known case. It could no doubt be argued by a constitutional lawyer that no infringement was committed by President Nkrumah either of the constitution or of the law. Strictly speaking, the same can be said of the South African government, which never departed by a millimetre from the constitution in suppressing the franchise of the Cape Coloured voters. Both were deplorable actions; but it is only against South Africa that that world is called upon to carry its indignation to the point of exercising economic sanctions—in which, incidentally, President Nkrumah refused to participate when they were first mooted in 1959, because South African trade was too valuable to Ghana.

The difference in the two cases lies, of course, in the South African assertion of white racial superiority, which is indeed abominable; but human rights ought not to be adjudicated in racial terms.

As it happens, it is almost exclusively as between the white and the non-white races that the dual standard applies. The Indian government may detain Indian political prisoners to a number exceeding the maximum ever held by the British in India, almost without reproach. An Indonesian official can declare his government's intention to civilise the people of West Irian 'at bayonet point if necessary', almost without a ripple of comment: the people in question are, ethnologically speaking, quite distinct, but the distinction is not between a white race and a coloured one.

When the newly independent government of Burundi took out of prison a group of political assassins (including Europeans) who had already been tried and sentenced, and tried them again and hanged them, not a single African leader uttered a word of protest. A European woman who complained that she had been tortured in a gaol in Tanganyika had half a column in the

Guardian devoted to her case, but what is that compared with the storm of publicity given to the misconduct of the Hola Camp in Kenya under British rule? The tendency is simply to expect and accept as a fact of international life that standards of justice will be lower in the newly emergent countries.

It may be that this expectation is false, and would be shown to be false on thorough investigation of many of the accepted stories. But the point is that it *is* the general expectation, and that is why the stories are accepted almost without comment. There are exceptions, of course, where public opinion has refused to accept such a dual standard; and these deserve mention, because public opinion is right, but they are few.

Two recent examples arose from the application of the Fugitive Offenders Act of 1881 to ex-British colonies. In the first case, the fear that standards of public safety might not prove adequate in a politically controversial murder-trial led to the refusal of the British government to return two Cypriots to Cyprus under the Act in 1962. The Act was invoked again with a different result in 1963, when the Nigerian government sought the return of Chief Enahoro. Public anxiety in this case arose from the fear that a political offender might not get a fair trial; and there was strong pressure in consequence for the amendment of the Fugitive Offenders Act, which was a survival from a period when the same system of law was common to the whole British Empire.

The operation of the Act had never caused any difficulty between Britain and the first independent countries of the Commonwealth, which were of course also British by descent. To amend the Act because of difficulties with the newer Commonwealth countries might therefore savour of the application of a dual standard by the British government, which has always been extremely reluctant to allow any hint of discrimination between two classes of Commonwealth membership. Whatever the outcome, it was a disquieting fact that a system of justice which had operated smoothly for many years between the members of the old 'white Commonwealth' should cause bitter complications within two or three years of independence with two members of the new Commonwealth. The dilemma in this particular case is that either to amend the law or to leave it unamended carries the risk of recognising a dual standard.

There are admittedly some respects in which the application of a dual standard has to be accepted as unavoidable. An instance can be readily seen by comparing what happened to two formerly British territories which were found to be economically non-viable as separate units: Newfoundland, the oldest British colony, and Nyasaland, a 19th-century protectorate. When Newfoundland proved unable to stand on its own legs as an independent Dominion, the obvious course on economic grounds was to merge it in Canada as an additional province; and this was done after the Second World War without too much heart-burning.

A few years later the economic argument of non-viability was invoked for merging Nyasaland with the two Rhodesias in the Central African Federation; but after ten unhappy years of trial the experiment had to be abandoned, although the economic benefits to Nyasaland were substantially proved. The reason for the breakdown was of course one which did not exist in the case of the white Dominion—racial incompatibility; and that had to be allowed to prevail over economic calculation.

Another example of the impossibility of a single, universal standard may be seen in the context of defence policy. In 1959 Mr Khrushchev made a proposal for universal disarmament, by the terms of which each country would reduce its armaments within four years down to the minimum level necessary merely for the maintenance of internal order. It was at once observed that this proposal would have had different consequences in the western and the Communist states: for example, Britain maintains no armed forces at all merely for purposes of internal order, whereas the Soviet Union's police forces are heavily armed, with tanks, artillery and aircraft among other weapons. This in itself made the proposal impracticable in a literal sense.

But the important point in the present context is not the disparity between the different kinds of major powers, but the disparity between the major powers collectively and many of the minor ones. In the case of such countries as Egypt, Indonesia or the Congo, to name only a few typical instances, the government itself could not remain in power without the support not merely of the forces of law and order but of the armed services themselves. The Khrushchev plan could therefore only have been applied to such countries by a sort of neo-colonialist intervention by the great powers themselves.

The dependence of many emergent countries on their armed forces can be seen in the long list of names of military rulers. Egypt, the Sudan, Iraq, Pakistan, Korea, and several of the Latin American republics, are now ruled by service officers; and in many other countries— for instance, Burma, Thailand, Laos, Syria, Lebanon, Iran, the ex-French and ex-Belgian Congo and again many of the Latin American republics—the armed forces are never far from the centre of the stage when changes of government take place, which is not infrequently. A recent example is South Vietnam.

Military government has an unpleasant sound in English ears, but it is not necessarily unpopular, and the circumstances in which it comes about are understand-

able. In a country which lacks political experience, because it has been under foreign rule, the armed services
are likely to provide not only the sole group of people
accustomed to disciplined and orderly administration,
but also one of the few opportunities of a career open to
all young men of the rising middle class. It is not surprising if they become intolerant of the inferior talents
of inexperienced politicians, and seek successfully to
usurp their positions.

The use of armed forces abroad affords another example of the dual standard. I pointed out earlier that
there was no serious reaction even in the western world
when India used force to take over Goa, or Indonesia
to take over West Irian. The same has been true of the
frequent threats of a number of African states, particularly at the Addis Ababa conference in 1963, to use force
against the Portuguese 'overseas provinces' of Angola
and Mozambique, or against Southern Rhodesia and the
South African Republic.

Such language or conduct on the part of a European
power is no longer conceivable to-day. Yet in the case of
Asian and African powers, not only does it excite little
comment: what is more, the same powers continue to be
regarded as possessing a special virtue, denied to the
major ex-colonial powers, in fulfilling the peace-keeping
role of the United Nations. India and Ghana remain
qualified for such a role, whereas France and Britain are
not; and this is accepted, however grudgingly, by the
French and the British as much as anyone else.

An illustration of the paradox in the case of India
occurred in 1961 when Indian forces were playing an
important role in the UN operation in the Congo. During the fighting to prevent the secession of Katanga, the
UN commander requested that the British government
should supply bombs for use in Canberra aircraft belong-

ing to the Indian Air Force. Although there had been accusations against the UN force of attacking hospitals and other civilian targets, the British government at first agreed, with some reluctance, to supply the bombs, and then shortly afterwards reversed its decision. The principal ground for the reversal was the appreciation that the Indians already had ample stocks of the required bombs; but it was widely attributed, in Britain as well as in Africa and India and at the UN, to the alleged machinations of a group of right-wing M.P.s and businessmen loosely known as the 'Katanga lobby'.

A few weeks after the incident, the Indians invaded Goa. But few people, even in Britain, publicly suggested that this might have been the eventuality for which the Indians were conserving their military supplies, while asking for replacements to use in the Congo.

It cannot be proved, needless to say, that this was the Indian government's motive. The point is that it was scarcely even suggested, as it would readily have been if (say) the French had been in the Indians' position. The essence of the dual standard in such a situation is that a less plausible but anti-colonialist explanation tends to be preferred to a more plausible explanation which might be damaging to the reputation of an uncommitted nation; and this preference has effect not only in Africa or Asia but equally among some influential sectors of public opinion in the ex-colonial countries themselves.

The *locus classicus* is perhaps that of the tragic accident in which Mr Hammarskjold, the Secretary-General of the United Nations, was killed in 1961, which is still widely believed, against all the evidence, to have been caused either by the British government or by Sir Roy Welensky on its behalf. Even among those who admit that the evidence will not bear examination, the opinion nevertheless survives that the British government was in some sense morally guilty of Mr Hammarskjold's death because it had not whole-heartedly supported the Congo operation. No such damaging opinions would have been expressed if (say) Nigeria had been in Britain's position.

An equally disturbing manifestation of the dual standard is its application by the newly emergent states to their relations with the great powers. It has long been apparent that they judge the actions of the USA, Britain and France on the one hand, and of the Soviet Union or Communist China on the other, by different criteria; and their attitude towards the latter is more tolerant than towards the former, at least until they learn otherwise by bitter experience.

The most familiar example to English readers of the application of a dual standard occurred in 1956 when the Anglo-French landing in Egypt coincided with the Soviet operation against the Hungarian rising. The reaction of the uncommitted nations, particularly India, then seemed grossly discriminatory in its condemnation of the two great-power interventions against small powers.

An equally striking example occurred in 1961, when the opening of a conference of the uncommitted nations in Belgrade coincided with the renewal by the Soviet Union of nuclear tests, which had been suspended by the three major nuclear powers since 1958. The criticisms of the Soviet Union by the heads of government assembled in Belgrade were notably muted. One of them openly admitted that it would have been quite otherwise if the first breach of the tacit truce had been made by the USA.

A disturbing feature of these occasions from the western point of view was that the inequality of the dual standard in this kind of context appeared to be growing greater. A few years earlier, at the Bandung Conference of the Afro-Asian states in 1955, it had looked as if the balance of criticism was more evenly held by the uncommitted nations between the great powers of the two *blocs*. Even close associates of the western powers, such as Turkey and the Central African Federation, were invited to Bandung (though the latter declined); and pro-western leaders such as the then Prime Minister of Ceylon, Sir John Kotelawala, had the opportunity to speak their minds vigorously against Communist imperialism. The leaders of the uncommitted nations, Mr Nehru pre-eminent among them, were clearly still feeling their way at that date towards a *modus vivendi* with both major power *blocs*. But five years later they appeared to have adopted a markedly anti-western conception of impartiality.

A few years later still, in 1962, Mr Nehru learned a painful lesson from Chinese aggression which caused him personally to revise his views very sharply. But it may be doubted whether this made much difference to the general application of the dual standard.

There are several reasons for such doubt. One is that the Chinese humiliation of India gravely damaged Mr Nehru's personal reputation, including his standing as the moral leader of the uncommitted nations as well as his prestige in India. It did so not only because it exposed his miscalculation of China's respect for the 'five principles' of peaceful co-existence, which he and the Chinese Communists had worked out at Bandung, but also because it exposed the inefficiency of India's defences and demonstrated afresh the principle already made familiar by European history, that the only successful neutrality is the neutrality of those who are strongly armed and determined to defend themselves.

There may be added two other reasons why it is doubtful whether the Chinese aggression made much difference to the general application of the dual standard. Although one Communist great power came badly out of the episode in the eyes of the uncommitted, the other Communist great power—the Soviet Union—came well out of it, by condemning China and offering help to India; and the USA did not come particularly well out of it either, because Chinese aggressiveness could still to some extent be blamed on the Americans' refusal to admit the People's Republic to the United Nations.

In the upshot, the characteristic reaction of the uncommitted states remains that of President Nkrumah at the time, which was to urge the rest of the world to refrain from intervening with effective help on either side between India and China, as though the balance of blame were equal between them.

It is a commonplace to say that the self-assertion and the dual standards of the new nations are understandable and excusable. No doubt they are; but they will become progressively less so as those nations become less new, and it should also be a commonplace to say that this is already happening. The ebullitions of newly emancipated nationalism will not always be readily tolerated.

Nationalism is a youthful affectation: it has been well compared to juvenile delinquency. But juveniles are expected to grow up. Countries can no more expect than human beings to have allowances made for them everlastingly on the grounds that they are youthful and have been through a hard time. It may be some time still before the change in public attitudes comes about. But the likelihood that it will eventually come about is all the greater because at the same time as the new states have been asserting their nationhood the tide of thought among the older nation-states has taken a new and opposite direction.

Nationalism in the old world, in fact, is on its way out.

5

The Obsolescence of the Nation-State

IT WOULD be grotesquely premature to declare national-ism defunct in the continent of its birth. That is belied by the passionate feelings of the Germans about re-unification, by the revived longing for the glory of France implicit in Gaullism, by the profound hostility of what was perhaps a majority of the British people to the idea of joining the Common Market; not to mention the hideous upsurge of nationalist frenzy in Central Europe between the world wars.

But there is none the less a strong and growing con-viction among the peoples of Europe that nationalism is not enough, that the nation-state is no longer adequate to the problems of the 20th century. Frenchmen and Germans are included in the forefront of this new wave of political thought, even if President de Gaulle and ex-Chancellor Adenauer are not. These are two of the great surviving nationalists, as fervent as Churchill; and al-though the tide is running against them, they have still been able to find under-currents within it which are favourable to their more old-fashioned purpose.

The reason for the trend away from nationalism in Europe since the Second World War lies partly, but only partly, in that war itself. Europeans became sick to death of what appeared in retrospect to have been a century of civil wars fought in the name of the nation-state. The primary object of the early stages in the European move-ment was to make another war between France and Germany impossible: that was explicitly declared by M. Schuman in putting forward his plan for what became the European Coal and Steel Community. The object, it can now be seen, has in fact been completely achieved, so that another war between France and Germany has become as unthinkable as another war between Britain and the USA.

It is just because the object has been so completely achieved that the movement towards integration has lost some of its momentum in recent years. The Franco-German treaty of 1963, negotiated by the two grand old nationalists, de Gaulle and Adenauer, marked in fact a step backwards in the European movement.

The opportunity to pursue nationalist ends even against the flow of the tide arises from the nature of the motives which are inducing the current movement away from and beyond the nation-state. The movement is not inspired by mere idealism, although idealism is strong among many of its advocates. It is inspired rather by the recognition of necessities — welcome necessities to those who are moved by the European ideal, but harsh necessities to those who are not.

These necessities make themselves felt in the related fields of defence, industry and commerce. In each case it was a sense of inescapable need, not an idealistic sentiment or an abstract desire for political experiment, which produced new institutions: the North Atlantic Treaty Organisation, the European Coal and Steel Community, Euratom, the European Economic Community or Common Market. The reasons are now long familiar: the European states saw firstly that they could not defend themselves singly against the Soviet Union, and secondly that they would all benefit from the economic strength of a larger unit than the traditional nation-state. The political sentiment supervened upon these calculations, but would not have been generated without them.

But the sense of need was still not sufficiently urgent or

overwhelming to carry them the whole way towards a new and supra-national political system, nor to carry the whole of western Europe even part of the way. NATO succeeded in attracting almost the whole of western Europe, but it did not abrogate national control of defence: the attempt to do that through the European Defence Community was a failure. The ECSC attracted only the six founder-members, although Britain later became associated with it; and the EEC likewise has so far remained limited to the six founders, although Greece and Turkey obtained treaties of association.

The belated attempt of Britain to join the EEC, along with other members of the European Free Trade Association, ended in a breakdown which incidentally exposed some of the weaknesses of the original structure of the Six and the shakiness of some of their premises. At the beginning of 1963 the European movement therefore suffered, on both sides of the English Channel, its severest setback since the collapse of the EDC nine years earlier.

The inclination in Britain and the USA was to blame the setback on President de Gaulle, who was certainly responsible for the decisive blows. But he too, like the European supra-nationalists, was responding to facts and not to personal whims. In the first place, he saw the British people as inadequately European in outlook: they interpreted 'interdependence' as a relationship which could be established with different people in different contexts (with the USA in defence and with the Commonwealth in economic development, for instance) instead of a comprehensive and exclusive relation with Europe. In the second place, he recognised that some of France's partners in the Six were showing signs of dissent from his conception of European unity, as witness their almost unanimous desire to bring Britain into it.

74

There were also some fields of national activity in which the sense of an imperative need for European unity was manifestly less strong than national interest. One of these was agriculture, in which the Six found it difficult enough to arrive at a common policy even without Britain; another was defence, in which de Gaulle insisted that it was impossible to have nuclear weapons under any but national control.

The setback of 1963, and the revival of traditional nationalism embodied in the elderly leaders of France and the German Federal Republic, naturally raised the question whether the sense of need which had given the European movement its practical impulse, as distinct from the philosophical sentiment which had generated the idea, had any staying power left in it. The answer is surely that it has, though European nationalism will undoubtedly die hard.

The forces which impelled the nation-states of western Europe in the 1950s towards collective defence and a Common Market at the expense of national sovereignty have in fact grown stronger, not weaker, in the 1960s. The trend has been masked to some extent by the fact that the same forces have provoked a nationalist reaction, of which President de Gaulle has made himself the popular figurehead. It is easy for such a reaction to achieve a temporary success, as it has done in France; but in the long run it is likely to prove as illusory as a conjuring trick.

I will take an example of the forces at work which has ramifications throughout the whole field of discussion. Defence and certain important sectors of industry are obviously closely related. Often defence production and civil production are in competition, for instance in their demands on skilled labour and scarce raw materials. Such competition can present serious problems to a country dependent on its balance of trade, as it did in Britain during the period of rearmament which began with the Korean War in 1950. But sometimes the needs of defence production and civil production are inter-dependent and even inseparable; and this has become in-creasingly the case with the development of more sophis-ticated weapons since the Second World War.

There is almost no civil application for the technology underlying conventional artillery or tanks; but the case is quite otherwise with aircraft and aero-engines, elec-tronics, rocket-propulsion or space-launching. In these cases it is impossible for even the wealthiest country to undertake the cost of the entire range of new develop-ments without the certainty of both a civil and a military market to sustain the spread of the overheads.

The rub comes when the point is reached, as it has long since been reached in the case of aviation, at which the size of the requisite market for the intended product, both civil and military together, exceeds the capacity of any one single nation-state that is engaged in such pro-duction. The point is naturally reached earlier or later according to the size and circumstances of each particular state: for Britain or France it comes much earlier than for the USA, for Italy or Belgium earlier still.

The USA, moreover, with its vast programme of over-seas aid, is in a stronger position to negotiate sales of its own products abroad as part of a bargain with countries receiving economic aid. As a result, Britain and France find themselves put in the position of being simultane-ously the allies of the USA in the context of defence policy and the competitors of the USA in the context of overseas trade in products closely related to defence. The policy of harmonising weapons production, which seems so rational from a political point of view, thus carries the danger for the lesser industrial countries of the alliance that their industries will be annihilated by US competition.

The natural reaction of the European states of the western alliance is to see that their only chance of meeting American competition on equal terms lies in partnership. Neither the British nor the French aircraft and electronics industries can by themselves find a sufficient domestic market on which to base an adequate overseas market such that the two combined will serve to spread the costs of research and development on a scale competitive with the corresponding US industries. The logical recourse is therefore to go into partnership.

The logic becomes most apparent in a particular and spectacular case, such as the development of a supersonic passenger transport aircraft. Both the French and British industries had ample experience of supersonic aircraft production from their military programmes, as had also the USA. But it was doubtful whether the world market would be sufficient to justify even two independent nationally-produced supersonic transports, let alone three. The natural step for the British and French governments to take, therefore, was to decide to pool their resources and produce a joint aircraft; and that is what they did.

The step was taken even under the presidency of de Gaulle, which is to say that it would certainly not have been taken if there had been any purely national alternative. His government also agreed to participate in other technological partnerships which no European nation-state could afford on its own, such as the project for a space-satellite launcher based on the abortive British weapon, Blue Streak. But the French President drew the line at co-operation in the control of nuclear weapons themselves. These, he insisted, must be purely national and independent: *'il n'y a de force nucléaire que nationale'* was his slogan.

It seemed all the more surprising that he should make his intransigeant stand at that particular point because it became apparent at the same time that even the USA and the Soviet Union, with far greater resources, were finding that a wholly independent programme of weapons development and space projects was beyond their capacity: hence, in part, the limited test-ban treaty of 1963. But de Gaulle, like Mao Tse-tung and a few others, would have none of it.

The reasons must be to some extent speculative, and it is only with those of the French that I am here concerned. In essence they are presumably similar to those which impelled the British Conservative government to maintain an independent nuclear deterrent, even when its critics argued that it was neither truly independent nor adequate to deter. There may be objective reasons going beyond those so often canvassed in the Press. Considerations of mere prestige perhaps play a smaller part in crucial decisions than is sometimes thought.

To see the crux of the matter, it is necessary to appreciate that the most vital element in military power is no longer the nuclear war-head alone: that can almost be described as a status-symbol, in itself relatively easy to achieve. What is increasingly important is the means of delivery, which can only be developed and continually improved by a first-class industrial power with enormous resources in skill and capital. In other words, to be a nuclear power to-day is in a sense a by-product of leading the world in science-based industries; and these industries are in turn essential to a country which makes its living by the export of increasingly sophisticated industrial products.

Naturally enough, neither Britain nor France nor any

other leading industrial power wishes to abdicate such leadership as it has obtained in these fields. The fact that the Americans urge them to do so, by giving up their pretensions to nuclear independence, is no inducement to conform: quite the contrary, as the British and French see it, because the only beneficiaries from such an abdication on their part would be the corresponding American industries.

What in fact seems likely to happen therefore is that Britain and France will continue to compete in the fields of advanced defence technology independently so long as they can, while recognising that the limit of what is nationally possible may one day be reached by both of them; so that when that day comes, and with it the inevitability of international partnership, their own national industries may be able to play a leading role instead of a subordinate one in the partnership.

The same considerations apply to the smaller of the industrially advanced countries of Europe, with the difference that they have mostly already reached, and recognised, the limits of what is nationally possible to them.

The example taken from the field of defence technology and the related civil industries, which is a very large and important field for an advanced national economy today, suggests that the pressures towards practical integration across national frontiers are likely to grow stronger rather than weaker. The idea of total independence based on the traditional nation-state is therefore unlikely to take on a new lease of life in Europe, even though momentary developments, such as President de Gaulle's assertion of French nationalism, may occur to suggest otherwise.

As a matter of fact, even de Gaulle's conduct in 1963 does not really imply a reversal of the trend: it was rather a recognition of that trend and a claim to French hegemony over it. The reason why it was unpopular with other Europeans was because they do not want any nation as such to play a predominant role in the new Europe when it emerges. For them the lesson of the Nazi unification of Europe between 1940 and 1945 was that no nation should play such a role, not that some other nation is to be preferred in it to Germany. In other words, they have recognised as a matter of hard necessity, not merely of sentiment, that supra-nationalism entails an element of national self-sacrifice.

At the moment the realisation involves a certain impatience with the French, as it did also for many years with the British. But in both cases that impatience is likely in the long run to pass away as inexorable circumstances bring the last of the great nationalists gradually into line. What will then remain and probably grow, however, is a similar impatience with the very large number of other countries in the world which have not yet had to learn the same harsh lessons, but which have on the contrary been taught by the tolerance of their former masters that there are virtually no limits to the nationalist self-assertion of the newly independent.

Here lies the strange and crucial paradox of the 20th century: that while the traditional nation-states are being remorselessly driven to the conclusion that national sovereignty is an obsolete concept, more and more new peoples are pressing forward, permitted and encouraged by the traditional nation-states themselves, to acquire precisely that same status. Such a paradox can surely not endure indefinitely.

How will the paradox work itself out? At present there is a disequilibrium between the old and the new in the emergent concert of nations, which may be summarised thus: the traditional nation-states have had to endure the full consequences of national independence and unrestricted sovereignty for many generations, and they find them increasingly intolerable; the new states are still sheltered from the impact of those consequences, so that they enjoy the fruits of national independence without the full responsibilities of it. The traditional nation-states are seeking to evolve a new system of international relations while encouraging the new states to emerge into the old one. At the same time, uneasily aware of the paradoxical and even self-contradictory character of the situation, they try to induce a more responsible attitude in the new states by alternately coaxing and chiding them.

Neither alternative is effective. In the long run, there can only be one effective way of rectifying the disequilibrium, which is to treat the new states as fully mature and responsible and to expose them to the full consequences of independence.

If that is not to be a catastrophic process, it cannot be done ruthlessly or instantly, without preparation. It cannot be done, for instance, in the old-fashioned way by force: that would mean a recrudescence of imperialism, which would be unacceptable and intolerable in the current mood of world opinion, even if it were an act of collective instead of national imperialism, such as the United Nations came near to committing in the ex-Belgian Congo.

Nor can it be done by calculated economic pressures, although many of the new states believe that this is in fact the policy of the ex-imperialist powers already, and label it 'neo-colonialism'. It is doubtful whether any example can be found in history of political changes being induced in one country by another country or countries purely by deliberate economic pressures. That is why it was idle to invoke them against the Nationalist government of South Africa; and if they could not be invoked against Dr Verwoerd it would be unthinkable to invoke them against any of the newly emergent countries. There is in fact no short cut to the promotion of national maturity and international responsibility.

The process of adjustment must be an evolutionary one, and the onus of it must lie primarily on the newly emergent countries. They have to learn the facts of international life for themselves. Some have to learn to adopt respectable economic and trading practices; some have to learn to tolerate legitimate opposition and to respect civil and human rights; some have to learn to do as they would be done by in their relations both with their neighbours and with the rest of the world; some have to learn that the fact of having once been oppressed and humiliated does not confer an indefinite licence to behave arrogantly and irresponsibly; and most of them have to learn that the dual standard of international judgment will not be tolerated for ever.

The most difficult and most essential part of the lesson is that once warfare is eliminated as the natural solvent of incompatibilities national independence entails international responsibility, which in turn entails a readiness in the last resort to subordinate national self-interest to a wider requirement. Such a lesson can only be learned gradually and by experience.

I have presupposed in the last few paragraphs that war can be excluded as a means of altering the disequilibrium, or indeed of achieving anything else in the modern world. This is an important assumption, which not everyone is prepared to make. I have made it, however, for two reasons. The first is that if no such assumption is made there seems little point in continuing this kind of discussion at all: the alternative consequences on any other assumption are, if not unthinkable, at any rate so vast and fearsome as to require another and quite different kind of book. The second reason, in case the first seems merely evasive, is that I regard the assumption as demonstrably correct, insofar as any proposition about the future can be demonstrated at all. I shall argue it briefly and parenthetically, before returning to the main theme.

To start with a proposition which is unlikely to be contested: nuclear weapons have made warfare an unprofitable way of settling quarrels between the major powers which possess them. Therefore no major nuclear power is likely to start a war deliberately against another such power, except under the leadership of a madman. One cannot waste time on the hypothesis of madmen controlling the governments of major powers, since on that hypothesis no conceivable foreign policy can be devised except preventive war.

There remain three much-canvassed possibilities: firstly, war by accident; secondly, a minor outbreak of local hostilities spreading into a major, general war; thirdly, war deliberately started by a major non-nuclear power, such as Communist China. I believe all three dangers to be unreal, though the third comes nearest to reality, at any rate for the time being.

War by accident would be unexampled in human history; and it is in fact much harder to have an accidental disaster with nuclear weapons than with any others yet invented, as witness the fact that there have been quite a few accidents involving nuclear weapons since the Second World War without a single nuclear explosion being caused by them. But what is more probably meant is war by miscalculation, which is quite another matter. Miscalculation means not that the initial act of war is unintended (which would be an accident) but that its actual consequences are unintended; and that is probably the commonest of all causes of modern war. All that can be said about it briefly here is that, although it can never be ruled out absolutely, the cost of such miscalculations has now been made prohibitively high by modern weapons.

War by miscalculation would, of course, be rendered more likely, not less likely, by either premature or unilateral nuclear disarmament, such as is advocated by those who profess to be most gravely afraid of it; for premature nuclear disarmament would put the clock back to 1939, and unilateral nuclear disarmament would restore the conditions which made possible the only deliberate nuclear attack that has ever occurred, in 1945.

The second possibility is one which has to be taken seriously on historical grounds, since the expansion of small wars into great ones has been hardly less common than the case of war by miscalculation. But there is now a new factor in the situation which did not exist a generation ago. Modern weapons, even the so-called conventional ones—tanks, artillery, aircraft—are now so complex and expensive that no small power can afford to produce a full apparatus of war out of its own industrial resources. So the small powers buy their more sophisticated conventional arms from the major powers, which are also incidentally, in the main, identical with the nuclear powers.

But such a transaction is not completed with the payment and delivery, since the weapons require a continuing supply of spare parts, ammunition, and technicians; and such supplies can be cut off at short notice. Therefore the purchase of modern arms, even without a formal treaty, involves a binding link upon the recipient country, which cannot pursue an aggressive policy for long without the approval, or at least the acquiescence, of the supplying power; and the supplying powers are, *ex hypothesi*, those most anxious to avert a general war.

The limitation is even stronger if the weapons are accompanied by a loan to pay for them; and if a small power receives weapons from more than one major power its capacity for aggression is rather decreased thereby than increased. In consequence, during the last fifteen years, although there have been many local crises and outbreaks of a kind which used once to lead to a general war, they have all been successfully isolated and contained.

There remains the third possibility, that of war precipitated by a major, aggressive, but non-nuclear power such as Communist China. The danger is clearly real, at least for the time being, but it is not over-optimistic to look sceptically at it.

The aggressiveness of Communist China is plainly related to an inferiority complex. It arises partly from the world's refusal of recognition, whether the recognition refused is of the boundaries claimed by China or of the government itself; and partly from the lack of the industrial apparatus of a first-class power, including nuclear weapons. So far the inferiority complex has not led to the launching of a general war, though the world has perhaps escaped it only by a hair's breadth. Some comfort can be drawn from the evidence of rational calculation shown by the Chinese Communists in accepting a stalemate in Korea and in refraining from pushing the invasion of India too far. But what of the future, when they have nuclear weapons?

Nobody doubts that eventually the Chinese will develop nuclear weapons, even though the Russians have refused to help them. But nothing could be more sobering than the experience of acquiring nuclear power: it will be an immense drain on China's industrial resources, it will be psychologically satisfying to the Chinese, and it will teach them an unforgettable lesson about the facts of international power. No country that has so far acquired nuclear capacity has grown more aggressive as a result—quite the contrary. There is no reason to suppose that China's experience will be different; but of course that does not mean that the Chinese, in their present mood, should be given nuclear weapons, since that would deprive them of all the truly salutary lessons of the experience, leaving them only with the horrible advantages of it.

One other contingency needs to be mentioned for the sake of completeness. It is that war might begin on the frontiers which divide several countries, formerly united, between two hostile governments. The countries in question are Germany, China, Vietnam, Korea; and many Arabs would add Palestine. But on examination all of them turn out to be special cases of the three categories of danger already described. Germany (including Berlin) falls into the first category, China and Formosa into the third, the remainder into the second.

They are probably in each case the most sensitive and dangerous examples in their respective categories, but they do not differ in kind from the rest. The incentives to avoid disaster are the same in these special cases as in the generality of cases. No one can say for certain that disaster will be indefinitely avoided, but the probabilities are that it will; and probabilities are all that one can hope for. To proceed on any other assumption is, in the case of a study of this kind, to abdicate the task of proceeding at all. In the last remaining chapter, therefore, I exclude the possibility of war.

6

The Emerging Concert

HOW IS THE disequilibrium between the old and the
emergent states to be adjusted?

It is easy to describe the nature of international relations once that adjustment is achieved. We shall then
have a world in which all states, regardless of their size
and their history, are judged by the same standards; in
which it will no longer be necessary to discriminate in
favour of any people on any grounds in order not to be
accused of discriminating against them; in which internal
self-criticism by an informed public opinion will be as
natural in (say) Ghana or Indonesia as in Britain; and
in which the permanence and stability of the newer states
will be taken for granted. Such a situation is obviously a
long way off; but then it was a long way off in the 17th
century in Britain and France, and much more recently
still in Russia and the USA.

The main burden of the process must inevitably fall
on the new states themselves. But fortunately there are
also means by which the traditional nation-states can
help the process forward without putting intolerable
burdens on themselves. The means lie in the international
institutions through which independent states now trans-
act much of the business that was formerly transacted
either by diplomacy or by war. There are innumerable
such institutions, formed on a geographical or a func-
tional basis, in almost all of which (with the exception
of the few specifically confined to Europe) the new states
as well as the old participate. It is on them particularly
that we have to rely.

Britain is especially fortunate and well-placed in having one of the most effective institutions through which to operate, in the Commonwealth. Obviously the Commonwealth is unreproducible, but it is none the less important to assess its peculiar merits. Although selective, it is geographically world-wide: multi-racial, multi-lingual, multi-religious. Unlike other institutions, it never decides anything by a formal vote, so that a real consensus of opinion has to emerge by a process of give-and-take. And functionally it is comprehensive: it has a political, an economic, a cultural, and even a strategic aspect. But important as these all are, the importance of each is limited, and none of them supplies the specific cohesion of the Commonwealth.

Politically, the cohesion of the Commonwealth has been steadily attenuated since the Statute of Westminster, which was itself the recognition of an attenuation that had already occurred. The single sovereignty of the Crown has disappeared. Whereas in 1914 the King could declare war on behalf of the whole British Empire at a stroke, in 1939 he could only do so on behalf of the United Kingdom, the Indian Empire, and the remaining colonies; and of the rest of the Commonwealth, Eire remained neutral throughout and South Africa declared war only after a change of government.

To-day more than half the member-states are declared neutrals. Only the symbol of the Crown as Head of the Commonwealth remains: to recognise that is to be a member of the Commonwealth and to renounce it is to leave the Commonwealth, although to become a republic is not necessarily to do so. Moreover, many member-states have succeeded in departing radically from the British model of government—which may be described as parliamentary democracy based on a universal franchise and operated through two or more parties—without having

88

to leave the Commonwealth. Perhaps only a universal respect, at least in theory, for the rule of law can be regarded as a necessary and irreplaceable qualification.

The economic cohesion of the Commonwealth might be expected to be more durable because of its practical grounding in self-interest. In many ways however the pattern of economic relations no longer corresponds in reality to the institutional forms, such as the system of Commonwealth preference, or the Sterling Area with its related complex of privileges. Since Commonwealth preference consists of a system of bilateral treaties, it is possible to retain it in the case of countries leaving the Commonwealth, such as South Africa; and it is possible for new member-states, anxious to protect their nascent industries, to decline to concede any preferences at all, as many do, particularly those in Africa.

The Sterling Area too is neither an exclusive nor a comprehensive feature of the Commonwealth. There are non-members of the Commonwealth inside the Sterling Area (Burma, Kuwait, Ireland, Iceland) as well as the important exception of Canada outside it; and some of the new member-states which are large earners of foreign currency (Nigeria or Malaya, for instance) could easily afford to leave the Sterling Area if they chose. The fact that they do not so choose shows that the benefits of the system are real, but they cannot be complacently taken for granted.

It was believed by many that the economic cohesion of the Commonwealth, and therefore the very institution itself, would be irretrievably compromised by the British government's negotiations to join the European Economic Community. The stark choice was posed: Commonwealth or Common Market? But this picture of the choice was deceptive, if not an exact reversal of the truth.

There were good reasons for thinking that in reality

the choice lay not between the Commonwealth and the Common Market but between both and neither. The reason was not simply the ostensible one that Britain by joining the Common Market would become richer and stronger, and therefore better able to help the under-developed countries of the Commonwealth. It was rather that the Commonwealth countries themselves all had important trading interests with the rest of the world—particularly western Europe—as well as with Britain; and that trade with Europe was becoming more important to them while trade with Britain was becoming relatively less important. This was a fact of the post-war world to which Britain's negotiations with the E E C represented a belated but probably inevitable reaction.

On that hypothesis, it is possible to contrast the consequences of Britain's joining and not joining the Common Market in the following terms. In either case, the growing importance of the European market to the Commonwealth countries—particularly the newer members, but less so in the case of the older members—would gradually lead them to want to enter into new trading arrangements with the E E C. If Britain were inside the E E C, she would provide the natural and familiar point of contact through which the Commonwealth countries could seek those new arrangements. If Britain were outside the E E C, they would have to be sought by each Commonwealth country separately, on its own, and at the expense of its existing relations with Britain.

Thus in the former case, Britain's membership of the E E C would lead to a progressive drawing together of the Commonwealth around her again in a new setting; in the latter case Britain's exclusion from the E E C would lead to the Commonwealth countries being attracted one by one out of her orbit.

The reason why this argument was not readily recognised at the time of the negotiations is that it applies less strongly to the older Dominions of British descent—and above all, hardly at all to New Zealand, the most beloved of all Britain's ex-colonies—than it does to the newer member-states of Asia and Africa. Consequently there was much opposition expressed to the negotiations by the older Dominions, anxious to ensure that their interests should not be overlooked; and it was echoed by the newer member-states—most of whom were likely to benefit rather than suffer from Britain's membership of the EEC—not for economic reasons but because they feared a revival of European colonialism.

The opposition of both elements in the Commonwealth, the old and the new, the white and the coloured peoples, the temperate and the tropical territories, was naturally taken up by their supporters in the United Kingdom, so that the government found itself equally strongly criticised from the right and the left. But in some form, at some date, the endeavour will surely have to be renewed; and it is to be hoped that it will then be seen more rationally as a step towards revitalising the Commonwealth, not towards compromising or destroying it.

There can be no question, however, of a tightly-knit, inward-looking, exclusive Commonwealth, either in the economic context or in any other. This is particularly true of the cultural cohesion of the Commonwealth, about which again there can be no complacency but which it is nevertheless possible to take active steps to promote and strengthen. Like any other ex-imperial power, the British have left strong traces of their cultural tradition behind them—all the stronger because English is a world-language, not merely the *lingua franca* of the Commonwealth. Innumerable institutions are based on

British models: parliaments, law-courts, universities, clubs, professional associations, all the media of communication.

English is the language of the Prime Ministers' Conferences and all other gatherings, as also of higher education and administration. It is even the only language in which Asians and Africans can complain to each other about British colonialism. These things cannot survive without retaining some English habits of thought embedded in them. The maintenance of the English language is one of the major long-term interests of British foreign policy.

But it is not of course a link confined to the Commonwealth. The English language belongs to the world and can be used—as it is by the Americans, for instance, and by international Communism—as the vehicle of an entirely non-British culture. Nor is its status universally secure even within the Commonwealth. It has to compete with other major languages: French in Canada, Greek and Turkish in Cyprus, Hindi and Urdu and Chinese and Malay in Asia. Although it is everywhere the language of higher education, most Asians and Africans get no more than primary education, which generally (though not always) has to be given in the vernacular; and that means hundreds of different vernaculars.

In some of the Asian countries there is pressure to have English deprived of its status as an official language, so that it would become no more than a widely-spoken second language, as in Scandinavia or the Netherlands. It would be a serious setback if this kind of agitation were to succeed, since it is an immeasurable advantage to the Commonwealth to have a common language in which to reach agreement, or—still more important—to reach disagreement.

It is important because there are so many serious subjects on which Commonwealth countries do disagree. They disagreed, for instance, about the recognition of the Communist government of China, about the crisis over the Suez Canal, about the departure of South Africa from the Commonwealth. How serious their disagreements can be may be illustrated by the speculation, which is certainly not totally unreasonable, that the disputes between India and Pakistan over Kashmir and the Indus waters might very well have led to war between any two countries that were not members of the Commonwealth. Yet none of these disputes has in fact disrupted the Commonwealth, and very few members have ever exercised their right of secession. It is certain therefore that there are tangible benefits in the institution and at least some common aspirations among its members. The most important of these is probably the quest for security in a troubled and uncertain world.

Security in this context has virtually nothing to do with defence or strategy. It hardly needs saying that there is no longer any common defence policy within the Commonwealth, although the British still like to believe that they continue to hold their strategic bases on behalf of the Commonwealth as a whole. Neutralism or non-alignment is the foreign policy of a numerical majority of the member-states; and even among those which are not neutral, there is little compunction about entering into defence agreements with other powers to which Britain is not a party, as Australia, New Zealand, Canada and Pakistan have all done with the USA.

Nevertheless there is a sense, quite divorced from military significance, in which security is the common aspiration of all member-states of the Commonwealth. It arises directly from the paradoxical situation which I have already described, in which the traditional nation-states are seeking new and larger combinations while at the same time more and more, and smaller and smaller, new states are crowding forward to achieve the very status which their seniors regard as obsolete.

In this strangely contradictory situation, the Commonwealth provides a kind of halfway house for its members, between being swallowed up into some vaster aggregation on the one hand and having to stand alone in a dangerous world on the other. It confers, in the words of a former Prime Minister of New Zealand, Mr Peter Fraser, not independence with something subtracted from it but independence with something added to it. That addition is the sense of security. It is not necessarily a sense of security only against potential enemies, though that is certainly felt by members who are near neighbours of the Communist powers. It may be a sense of security against basically friendly but overpowerful neighbours, or even against other members of the Commonwealth.

An example of the former case is the relation of Canada or the West Indies with the USA; of the latter, the relations between India and Pakistan or between whites and blacks in Africa. For such purposes, and for the steady and rational adjustment of the disequilibrium between large and small states, between the old and the new or the advanced and the under-developed, it is difficult to conceive a more satisfactory institution than the Commonwealth.

But the Commonwealth is an accidental product of historical circumstances which cannot be repeated or extended. Even for its own members, it cannot be the sole institution through which the international disequilibrium is adjusted and the concert of nations reconstructed on a wider base. Nor can any of the other partial institutions, though they all have a part to play.

It is easy to see as a matter of theory that what is

wanted is a new system to take on the general role once played by the old concert of nations, making allowance for the fact that there is now a vastly wider spectrum of more nearly equal states. Some idealists believe that the only ultimate solution is a world-government, but that seems over-ambitious and unnecessary; and it would in any case probably not prove to be the end of the road. A more modest and practical self-regulating mechanism would be preferable; and this, as it happens, is exactly what we already have ready to hand, in the United Nations.

Some of the powers which founded the U N have subsequently adopted very short-sighted attitudes towards it. The most evident fact about it, which they have been reluctant to accept, is that it has come to stay, like the new states which now form its numerical majority. One has only to compare its history with that of its predecessor at the same age to see how solidly based and durable an institution the United Nations really is.

There were sixty-three members of the League of Nations at different times in its short life, but there was never a moment when all sixty-three were members simultaneously. Governments came and went as it suited them. The USSR was expelled without caring; and not only Germany and Japan, but many of the Latin American and Balkan States, resigned from it as a matter of no great consequence. It is inconceivable now that the same thing should happen to the United Nations, which already numbers well over a hundred members. Despite many idle threats of withdrawal, no member has ever yet resigned, and the only country which gave up its seat voluntarily (Syria) was quick to recover it again at the first opportunity.

Several of the founding governments nevertheless talk in moments of disenchantment as if the United Nations

95

were expendable, or at any rate susceptible of radical reconstruction so that it could be restored to its 'original purpose'. There was in fact provision in the Charter for its revision after ten years, but when the time came in 1955 there was no hope of any agreed reforms. What had happened, however, was that certain evolutionary changes had taken place by a process of trial and error and by the growth of case-law, which is exactly what was to be expected of any healthy organism.

The most important of these changes all tended in the one direction of strengthening the influence of small powers at the expense of great powers. For instance, the so-called 'veto' of the five great powers in the Security Council was weakened by the ruling that abstention did not constitute a veto; and the 'Uniting for Peace' resolution in 1950 considerably increased the stature of the General Assembly. The second Secretary-General, Mr Dag Hammarskjold, deliberately encouraged the trend away from great-power hegemony, thus incidentally increasing the authority of his own office.

These developments were equally unwelcome to all the great powers which had founded the UN, but were accepted with the least fuss and the most judicious far-sightedness by the USA. The reason is no doubt in part that the US government has relatively few major concerns of the kinds most likely to attract UN intervention, which fall mainly into three categories. They are, firstly, problems of de-colonisation; secondly, such matters of domestic jurisdiction as are also matters of international interest; thirdly, the protection of vital national interests abroad.

In the first two categories, the Americans have had almost no trouble at all with the UN, though they have perhaps been lucky to escape interference in the question of civil rights for American negroes. In the third category, the US government has generally handled its problems—the Truman Doctrine and the Korean War, for instance, and even the Cuba crisis of 1962—not only with a firm regard for national interest but also with at least a tactful respect for the UN Charter. The European powers, on the other hand, have tended to be more impatient and cavalier in their dealings with the UN.

Such behaviour seems to be short-sighted, given that the UN has come to stay, as it undoubtedly has, and that the numerical majority in it is always going to lie with the newer states. Once the process of de-colonisation is complete, which must mean well before the end of the present century, there will be two major interests for the European powers to safeguard: one is that the new states should behave responsibly both at home and abroad; and the other is that no new imperialism (Chinese, for example) should replace the defunct imperialism of Europe.

There is no other instrument besides the UN, either in existence or in prospect, through which those two interests could be safeguarded; and they can only be safeguarded through the UN if in the meantime the founder-members of the organisation treat it with the utmost respect, so that a strong international public opinion is built up in favour of responsible policies and against purely self-regarding actions. This entails a severe and sometimes painful self-discipline on the part of the older states; but then self-discipline is exactly what they want to induce in their juniors.

It does not mean, as some of the simpler-minded champions of the UN in Britain seem to think, that the British government or any other has an obligation invariably and uncritically to vote with the majority. There is nothing reprehensible about being in the minority. It is as much a duty at the UN as at Westminster to state one's case and vote for it. What would be reprehensible would be, having voted with the minority, to seek to frustrate the action decided upon by the majority.

Here there is a difficulty which does not occur in the functioning of national democracies, in that the executive branch of the UN, insofar as it has any, consists of the whole membership collectively. In a national parliament the opposition, having been defeated in a division, is expected to acquiesce in a decision of the majority but is not called upon to participate in the execution of it. In the UN the member-states collectively are the executive, so that the self-discipline of the minority may find itself under severe strain. That was, of course, the reason for introducing the principle of the 'veto'; but the veto does not exist in the General Assembly, which has gradually been acquiring a predominance at the expense of the Security Council.

As a matter of practical politics, therefore, the dissenting states, or those against whose interests action is intended, are not called upon to take an active part in the execution of decisions. The British and French governments (though not, strictly speaking, dissenting) were not invited to contribute to the UN Emergency Force in the Middle East, for instance; nor were any ex-imperial powers invited to participate in the Congo operation. But that is just the trouble. It follows that the governments which regard themselves, not without reason, as the most mature and responsible tend to be specifically excluded from the most delicate operations of the UN, and sometimes (as in the Congo) to be accused of sabotaging those operations even as non-participants. They in turn regard the conduct of the new, small states in such operations as immature and irresponsible.

It is highly desirable that such suspicions should be removed, which will inevitably be a slow process. It can only occur at all if the older states set an example of faithful and unquestionable acquiescence in all majority decisions of the UN, even those which they have publicly criticised and voted against.

Another consideration which makes the necessary self-discipline painful is that the wealthy minority in the UN is still going to have to continue providing economic aid to the under-developed majority, even while it submits to that majority's unwelcome political decisions. Nothing can make this prospect appetising, except a very long-term view of the good of humanity. It requires painful adjustments of thought. It involves, in the first place, abandoning many of the conceptual dichotomies of the Cold War, such as the contrast between the so-called 'free world' and Soviet tyranny, or between peace-loving socialism and war-mongering capitalism. But these ideas are so ludicrously irrational that they must eventually wither away of their own accord, as they are perhaps just beginning to do. There are other more difficult changes to be faced.

The self-discipline of the richer and senior members of the UN will also involve tolerating all sorts of intolerable things: enduring taxation without control over the use of the proceeds; accepting that corruption is a highly probable and perhaps ultimately healthy feature of the under-developed economies; allowing secondary industries in the advanced countries (textiles in Britain, for instance) to decline for the benefit of similar industries in the new countries; allowing the new countries to establish dictatorships and even to go Communist (or, of course, anti-Communist) on the proceeds of foreign aid; and so on.

There will always be powerful short-term arguments against doing any of these things. They will, nevertheless, continue inevitably to be done for so long as they are necessary, until the beneficiaries are self-supporting. They will be done on the basis of various long-term calculations. One of these is, on the western side—and presumably *vice versa* on the Communist side—that if we do not do it, the other side will; and the under-developed countries will then drift into the opposite camp, whichever that may be. The reasoning is fallacious, as experience has often shown, but the result is not unsatisfactory; for it is desirable in the general interest that a major under-developed country such as India should not become a member of either camp, and therefore should enjoy economic aid from both.

Another long-term calculation is that the under-developed countries comprise the most important markets for future exports, once they have 'taken off' into self-sustained economic growth; and this is a valid argument. It is also true that in the present mood of world opinion it would be as unthinkable to refuse to help under-developed countries as it would be to abolish, say, the Welfare State in Britain; and there is not the slightest inkling of that mood changing yet. But the most important consideration ought probably to be that if we expect the new countries to develop a sense of international responsibility themselves, that is how we ought to behave towards them.

It is no idle hope that the new countries will develop such a sense of international responsibility in their economic relations, because examples can be quoted to show that some are already doing so. The first signs are naturally of solidarity between the ex-colonies against their ex-rulers. A specific instance was the help offered by Ghana to Guinea when the French brusquely terminated all their responsibilities there upon independence. More general instances are the various projects for 'common markets' in Africa, the Middle East and Latin America, in imitation of the European model.

There are also already signs of a more sophisticated stage approaching. One is the Organisation of Petroleum-Exporting Countries, which exists to protect the interests of those countries in all the continents against their European and American customers, although their interests as producers are also highly competitive against each other. It would be encouraging to see the same spirit animating the reactions of Britain's former colonies in Africa to the EEC; if they were to argue, for instance, that although Britain's membership of the Common Market would help tropical producers in Africa, it might hurt tropical producers in Latin America. But there is little sign yet of that kind of maturity.

A still more sophisticated stage is reached when the under-developed countries begin to recognise that it may be in the general interest for them to accept aid in a form which suits the convenience of the donor more immediately than that of the recipient. As one would expect, the outstanding examples come from India. Indian planners have more than once gone to the trouble of ascertaining what goods it would be most convenient for their benefactors to supply before asking for aid in precisely those forms. They have also abandoned the doctrinaire socialism of anti-colonialism, in favour of a recognition that it is to their national advantage to have foreign capitalists come in and (in old-fashioned jargon) 'exploit' them.

Such ideas are arriving only much more slowly in ex-British Africa, where foreign capital is still being frightened away by vague (and always unfulfilled) threats of nationalisation. But this time-lag is no cause for despair: rather one must be encouraged by the example of India, remembering her great prestige in the Afro-Asian world, and, for this reason among many others, redouble the efforts to ensure her survival and success in the world.

If some of the emergent states show fewer signs of maturity in political than in economic relations, this is not surprising: misguided emotions die much harder than miscalculations of material interest. But it may be that signs which are already there are less easy to see, for the same reason: and it may be that the adjustment of the disequilibrium and the emergence of a new concert of nations are nearer than we think.

At any rate, it can do no harm and may do much good for the older powers to act on this assumption. It is surely to be expected of Britain in particular, as the senior member of a society founded on the principle of political equality despite economic inequality. Every British government feels the obligation, none the less sincerely for occasional lapses, to set a disinterested example in their Commonwealth relations on the basis of that principle. It would be inconsistent to abrogate the principle in the wider society of the United Nations, where it also applies.

To require such an example of Britain in particular is to expect something which is often exasperating and which will sometimes seem not only contrary to our national interests but positively damaging to innocent people for whom we are responsible: Southern Rhodesia is a painful case in point. It can only be justified in the light of the long-term advantages of promoting, by our own example, the creation of a responsible and mature international society.

But there are also cases where it could be advantageous to British interests even in the short-term to place responsibilities firmly on the shoulders of the United Nations before any kind of effective agitation has been worked up about them. There are difficult relics of the former British Empire, particularly some of the smallest islands and coastal appendages, to which this argument would apply; and it is certain that sooner or later, if the initiative is not taken on our part, such agitation will be initiated against us.

One other thing is also certain in the long run. It is that, whether or not the kind of attitudes which I have been discussing are consciously adopted by the traditional nation-states, the process of adjusting the present disequilibrium will go on and the new concert of nations will emerge. On the presupposition which I have made, that the pattern of sovereignty at present prevailing in the world will not be upset by war, there is no other alternative but the continuation of this process towards its ultimate culmination.

It will, moreover, in any case seem a slow and painful process. All that is at issue is whether it shall be slow or very slow, painful or very painful. I do not pretend that the decision rests exclusively with the great powers or the traditional nation-states, because I have already argued that to a great extent the onus lies on the emergent peoples. But it does lie within the limits of our remaining powers to expedite or to hinder it.